DEAR MEN

DEAR MEN

MASCULINITY AND MODERN LOVE IN #METOO INDIA

PRACHI GANGWANI

BLOOMSBURY
NEW DELHI • LONDON • OXFORD • NEW YORK • SYDNEY

BLOOMSBURY INDIA
Bloomsbury Publishing India Pvt. Ltd
Second Floor, LSC Building No. 4, DDA Complex, Pocket C – 6 & 7,
Vasant Kunj, New Delhi, 110070

BLOOMSBURY, BLOOMSBURY INDIA and the Diana logo
are trademarks of Bloomsbury Publishing Plc

First published in India 2021
This edition published 2021

ISBN: PB: 978-93-90077-32-8; eBook: 978-93-90077-34-2
2 4 6 8 10 9 7 5 3 1

Typeset in Bell MT Std by Manipal Technologies Limited
Printed and bound in India by Thomson Press India Ltd.

MIX Paper FSC FSC® C010615

To all the men who broke women's hearts. Without you, there would be no need for a book like this.

CONTENTS

Introduction

As the sex and relationships writer for a leading women's lifestyle magazine, I'd often strike conversations about dating, sex, love and marriage with my colleagues. The magazine catered to young women with a focus on heterosexual relationships. Thus, my questions, too, then were mostly to heterosexual women. For example:

Me: 'What's the worst date you've been on?'

Colleague one, while staring at her laptop: 'The one where the guy didn't show up only. Ha ha.'

Colleague two *leans back into her chair and uses this question as a prompt for an untimely break*: 'Hmm... there was this one guy who just refused to leave. I met him for coffee, and I wasn't into him. So, I told him I had to leave because I had to meet some friends. He tagged along! I had to sit at some random café and pretend my friends were running late.'

Here's another example:

Me: 'What's the weirdest thing a guy has ever said to you?'

Colleague one *laughs to herself before answering while staring at the laptop*: '"My ex did it better," *while* I was necking him.'

We stopped what we were doing and turned to her. It was their second date. A third didn't happen, obviously. She didn't care.

Here's another:

Me: 'What would you change about your boyfriend?'

This question, as it became apparent, required undivided attention. My colleagues were all women, save for one who would chime in every now and then with, 'Really? Women don't like that?' When a conversation about relationships necessitated a huddle in the middle of the bay, he would awkwardly plug in his headphones and pretend we weren't there.

Colleague one: 'He never wants to go anywhere with me. I'm friends with all his friends, but he makes no effort with my friends.'

Colleague two: 'Yeah, mine too. And he's so awkward around my family! We've been dating for years now, and he still keeps his distance from them.'

Colleague one: 'Oh, and he's still friends with all his exes. I don't get that.'

Colleague two: 'I think men in general just have a problem communicating. My boyfriend replies in monosyllables, and it drives me crazy. I get so annoyed.'

Colleague one: 'Yeah, and conversation is sometimes so superficial. To him, everything is just okay. Like, nothing bothers him and that makes me feel like I can't talk to him about the things that bother me.'

Colleague three: 'This is why I don't want a boyfriend. Not worth it.'

Colleague three had had several dates in the past few months that didn't go anywhere. Some men ghosted her, some wanted to hook up with her but remain 'just friends'. One guy she went on a few dates with told her he was going on a vacation with some of his friends and returned engaged to his long-term girlfriend.

I'd have similar conversations with other groups of women — friends from college, friends of friends, strangers in ladies' washrooms pining over some guy who'd broken their heart. There is a lot of heartbreak among women, I realized, at the hands of men.

A year in, I decided that we needed a dating guide for men. That's how this book began. I already knew the kind of struggles women faced in relationships. I wanted to know what the other sex was going through. Were they confused about the rules of dating and relationships? Did they have any questions about dating that I could possibly address through this guide?

Promptly, I made a WhatsApp group that included 13 male friends and acquaintances. I started asking them questions: Did they think it was okay to ghost a woman? What kind of expectations did they think their girlfriends had of them? And they of their girlfriends? How did they deal with exes? Did they judge a woman based on the way she dressed? Whom did they think should pick up the tab on a date? Did they think a date was a go ahead for sex? I also started these conversations on social media (Instagram and Facebook), asking men to share their experiences. Both men and women responded to my questions. Over the course of nearly three years, I spoke to 71 men and 23 women about love and gender. While not all conversations have been included in the book, each one has informed the narrative. Also, while some of the learnings and observations in the book apply to both men and women, exploring the nuances for women is beyond the scope of this book, since this book is about masculinity and modern love, and has been excluded.

I have to say, I wasn't prepared for the kind of candour men brought to the table.

When I started having these conversations with men, I realized that a dating guide written by a woman for men would gather dust, not readers. More importantly, it defeated the purpose of this book. I wanted the book to redefine the role men play in romantic relationships and dos and don'ts wouldn't achieve it.

In the last few decades, the women's movement has gained momentum. In 2015, college students filed a petition to make hostel and paying guest (PG) accommodations less restrictive for women. Rightly named Pinjra Tod (meaning 'break the cage'), this movement aimed to challenge the belief that women need to be protected.[1]

Gulabi Gang, unofficially headquartered in Badausa in Uttar Pradesh, is a good example of the gnawing gap between law and culture. In India, cultural beliefs take precedence over the laws. While domestic violence was criminalized in the year 2005, it still exists.[2] Tired of the apathetic response of the police to complaints of domestic violence, Sampat Pal Devi took matters in her own hands and formed a vigilante group called Gulabi Gang.[3] The horrific gang rape of Jyoti Singh in December 2012 triggered many public protests, and

---

[1] Iyer, Aishwarya, 'Who Are Pinjra Tod & Why Did They Join CAA Stir?', *The Quint*, 29 May 2020

[2] The Protection of Women from Domestic Violence Act, 2005

[3] Dileep, Ganesh, 'Gulabi Gang: Breaking The Ceiling With Lathis', *Feminism In India*, 20 March, 2019

changes in the laws around crimes against women.[4] The #MeToo movement, in light of which this book was conceived, finally lifted the veil from workplace sexual harassment.[5]

All this while, men have been on the periphery of this gender revolution. While women have been breaking out of the mould of the patriarchy-prescribed idea of being 'feminine', and redefining what it means to be a woman, men have only begun to question the 'Man Box'. The Man Box is a term used for a set of rigid expectations and traits attributed to men. It reinforces a hegemonic definition of masculinity and promotes a sense of superiority to other gender groups, as well as superiority of some men over others. It leads to emotional suppression, misogyny and homophobia in men. Behaviours encouraged in this definition of masculinity include high risk-taking, being in a position of power over others, being in competition with other men, defining success based on money, and suppressing 'weak' or 'feminine' emotions such as sadness and fear.[6]

This gap in the exploration of gender roles has led to many unprecedented challenges in relationships. Women are now demanding that men be more emotionally available. A growing number of women are no longer financially dependent on men. I am a member of a women's only networking group in

---

[4] Correspondent, HT, '2012 Delhi Gang Rape Case: What Happened On December 16', *Hindustan Times*, 20 March, 2020

[5] Roy, Abhery, '2018: The Year When #MeToo Shook India', *The Economic Times*, 1 June, 2019

[6] Edwards, Keith, 'Man In A Box - The Traditional Definition Of Masculinity', *Keith Edwards*, 10 October, 2012. Greene, Mark, 'The Man Box: The Link Between Emotional Suppression And Male Violence', *The Good Men Project*, 2 October, 2018

which many have delayed marriage or motherhood to be able to focus on their career. When it comes to parenthood, many are no longer satisfied with a partner who is absent as a father. While women's expectations are changing, men are still processing the new role they are required to play.

Talking to women and men separately about the same issues made me realize something vital about modern love — we all want the same thing — to have a harmonious relationship, but our maps of getting there are starkly different. Women are discarding the old maps, and rewriting a new trajectory for their lives, while men have only begun to notice the roadblocks. We haven't bridged the gap when it comes to heterosexual love. The only way we can fix this is if we start talking *to* each other, instead of *at* each other.

The most important piece of this messy puzzle of modern love is listening.

Women often complain that men are terrible listeners. This may partly come from the fact that men and women have different listening styles. Men are 'action-oriented' listeners. This means when they are listening to someone talk about a problem, they are simultaneously looking for a solution. Women on the other hand, see conversation as an end in itself. Their solution is to feel heard and validated. This gap in listening styles has impacted relationships to the extent that it has become an Instagram trend. Of late, several reels have cropped up of women expressing their displeasure at their male partner abruptly offering solutions instead of simply listening.[7]

---

[7] Jansen, Corine, 'Sex Differences in Listening', Global Listening Centre

As a woman who consciously embarked upon this tumultuous journey of listening to men, I can tell you, it's not easy. I consider myself a good listener. An empathetic listener. I usually don't feel the need to offer solutions, and seldom pass judgements. But when the views of a group of people with whom one has to find a way to coexist are sometimes so antithetical to one's own, it's hard to continue listening without judgement or argument. Or offering solutions. But it's necessary. If we want heterosexual relationships to be more egalitarian, we must first understand why they're not.

This book is the first step towards gaining that understanding.

I spoke to men and women between the ages twenty and forty. It began with friends and acquaintances, and grew to friends of friends, acquaintances of friends, and the many men who responded to my incessant questions about love and relationships online. With some, the conversations didn't extend beyond a few text messages. With others, there were several voice and video calls. I met some men and have become good friends with a few. Some of the conversations happened organically at parties or get-togethers. Most of these men come from urban India — Delhi, Bengaluru, Mumbai, Chennai or have moved to big cities from tier two/three cities during early adulthood.

I consciously chose to speak to men living in urban India for a reason... I imagine that the kind of gender and relationship issues young men living in rural India face are remarkably different from men in urban India. Through some of the men I interviewed for the book, who had been raised in smaller towns, I learnt a few such differences. For example, in Mangalore, one quickly runs out of profiles to swipe on dating apps because there are so few young people who stay in the city after school. It's also almost impossible to meet someone outside of your circle because everyone knows everyone. So dating in Mangalore is a wholly different experience than dating in Bengaluru, where not only can you meet people from different walks of life, but also have some sense of anonymity. Although all tier one cities of India allow this sort of mobility and access when it comes to dating and relationships, the experience of dating in each city is unique. Those who've shuttled between Bengaluru and Delhi tell me that Bengaluru is much more laid-back than Delhi, and casual dating is easier there. In Chennai, the first date is usually a movie, unlike Delhi, where it's drinks and dinner.

India's diversity has also permeated its dating world. Yet, the men in our country are unified by their shared idea of masculinity. One word that repeated itself over and over again in my conversations with men was — stoicism. Men are raised to be stoics, to be unaffected by the vicissitudes of life, to remain unemotional in face of pain or joy. Many men view stoicism as a revered virtue and are proud to navigate life with equanimity. Most women see this lack of emotionality as a roadblock to intimacy. It's the same thing, but men and women have wildly different views about it. This book hopes to bridge the gap between many such conundrums of modern-day dating.

To get a better understanding of how masculinity manifests in relationships, I consulted Ayush Chandra, a clinical psychologist based in New Delhi. His therapeutic approach is gender affirmative and trauma informed, and his areas of expertise include substance use disorders, couples counselling, sexual therapy and mood disorders. From him, I learnt that emotional suppression among men is, indeed, a problem. Or in the very least, commonly leads to other problems and also impacts relationships. Through the course of this book, I will unpack how this happens.

During my conversations with Chandra, he often brought up the fact that India, and Indians, are in a transitional phase. That we are caught between the old and the new, between tradition and personal aspirations. Many of the men you will meet in this book are emotionally and intellectually divided when it comes to their role as romantic partners. While some of the stories may sound a bit extreme, this conflict between breaking out of the patriarchal 'man box' and staying within it is evident in most young men today.

Most names in the book have been changed to protect the privacy of the individuals. A few names have been retained, and of them, I'd like to mention two here who have given me valuable insights into the lives of men. Rajat Mittal, for helping me understand how the pressure to provide affects men, and Lokesh Pawar, for talking to me about the widespread sexual abuse of men and young boys.

A big chunk of this book was written after #MeToo came to India. While the movement gave women the mic and centerstage, it also made men think about their role in society. Men have mixed views about #MeToo. But the movement has certainly made it easier to talk about gender in the context of relationships. There was a palpable difference in the quality of my conversations with men before and after #MeToo. Not only was it less awkward to talk about consent and sexuality, there was also a new sense of urgency to talk about other aspects of relationships. Men spoke to me about the pressure to provide, being rejected, how confused they sometimes feel in relationships, and what they do when their needs aren't met. It was as if the movement had shown men that talking can help. And that talking about vulnerable issues is also a form of power.

The men I interviewed for the book are educated and internet savvy. They aren't unfamiliar with terms such as 'enthusiastic consent', or 'gender fluidity'. They aren't unaware of the current wave of gender dialogues that is urging men to be more in touch with their emotions and trying to take the pressure off them to fit into the traditional masculine roles of the 'muscular and successful' kind. But as I learnt, being equipped with a good vocabulary doesn't always mean that one understands the nuances of language. While men are trying to wrap their heads around this new, emerging masculine, there are some tactics they sometimes resort to, to deflect from the novelty of it all. One such tactic is humour. With many men, my first conversation with them about dating and relationships was usually met with wit and sarcasm. With gritted teeth, I'd laugh at their jokes to build rapport so that the next time I ask them what made them a good partner, they'd actually tell me. They would. Some men would talk to me at a hypothetical level: 'So this happened to a friend of mine…' or 'Most men do this, though…'

I listened to all these stories, and soaked them all in. There were many men who were like open books — candid and inquisitive. I thought long and hard about why some men were more in touch with themselves and open about their inner lives than others. There were two things common between these men; one, most of these men had either been in therapy or they deeply valued self-awareness, and two, they had been through some experience, either professionally or personally, that forced them to question their role as a man. Sadly, our education system, or even social interactions, don't inspire men to think about gender and relationships.

Slowly, though, things are beginning to change. Indian men in their twenties have more egalitarian values than men in their late thirties. They seem to be more gender neutral, and don't see working women or sexually active women as an oddity. At least on the surface. In just a few years, there has been a huge cultural shift from men expecting their partners to prioritize home over work to now expecting their partner to have a job and contribute financially; from men judging a woman's character based on her sexual history, to now, well, turning a blind eye to it.

There's progress, but we still have a long way to go.

I hope this book will inspire men and women to ask each other questions, sit back and listen to where we come from and where we want to go.

PART ONE

Masculinity

Modern Love, Masculinity and #MeToo

'It was a party, everyone was having fun, and I got a bit too drunk. Don't you ever get a little wild after drinking too much?'

—Suraj, thirty-five

IT WAS ONE of those rare occasions when I had gotten dressed on time and had ten extra minutes to while away before I had to leave for dinner. I stepped out on my balcony for a few quiet moments in the cool spring evening before hitting clutch-break in my heels. With another five minutes left, my phone rang.

My date's name flashed on the screen.

'Hey!' I answered, smiling into the phone.

'Hey! How's it going?'

'Good. I'm ready to leave. Will be out in another five minutes.'

'So…there's a slight change of plans. A couple of my friends want to meet you. I'll pick you up in half an hour, and we'll head together to where they are?'

'Oh,' the smile vanished from my face.

It had been five months since I first met my date. Not once had he picked me up. I had a car and would drive myself to see him every time. I had chauffeured him on occasions; I didn't mind that. He'd even been to my house and spent many nights over. Yet, I wasn't okay letting him have the reigns. We had usually met either in a neutral territory, or my territory.

'Guy friends?' I asked.

'Umm…yeah,' he answered, confused.

'Oh...' I paused to contemplate how to tell him that I didn't feel safe letting him pick me up for dinner with two other men. That I'd like to bring my car, so I could leave anytime I wanted. Without anyone else sitting next to me. 'Umm…that's okay. You don't have to pick me up. It'll be a detour for you. I'll see you there.'

He didn't argue or try to change my mind. He said okay and 45 minutes later, greeted me outside one of Delhi's most loved bars.

Not long before this evening, I had started writing about crimes against women in the country for the magazine. Every day, I'd read reports or wire articles about four to six cases of rape and molestation, and I'd have to pick any two to write about. Several of the reports I had read in the preceding months were of men raping women in moving cars. Once they'd have their fill, they would push her out of the car and leave her on the roadside.

So, when my date suggested he'd pick me up, the first thought that came to my mind was that after dinner and a few drinks, he and his friends would make me the next girl left on the roadside.

This was in May 2017. A few months later, in October 2017, stories of #MeToo started appearing in the news.

I realized I wasn't the only woman concerned for her safety while putting herself out there. Before #MeToo, women would do some sleuthing around on the Internet or Google every Tinder match before committing to a date, whereas now the movement equipped women with the vocabulary — and as a friend pointed out later, it also gave women courage — to talk about the things that had happened to us.

Love is a curious mix of adventure, attraction, desire, experimentation, rule-breaking, rule-making, flirtation...and fear. While deception may be as old as love itself, modern love comes with modern deception and modern fears. One of these is that the man who's caught a woman's fancy isn't all that he seems. That he doesn't actually walk the talk when it comes to gender issues, or equality. Words like 'woke' had already found their way to our vocabulary before #MeToo, but gender roles in love were still simmering under the surface. We knew we had to find a way to start talking about it, but it wasn't until #MeToo came to India that consent and gender bias became acceptable cocktail party topics, dinner table conversations and pillow talk.

9 October 2018. I was half-way through my first cup of coffee, barely awake, not yet ready for conversation, when my phone started buzzing with a barrage of WhatsApp texts. Names of my female friends started appearing one after another on the screen, which hadn't yet been unlocked. After the thirteenth or fourteenth message, from the sixth or seventh friend, I swiped up to see what the ruckus was all about.

The news was that Bollywood actress Tanushree Dutta had accused Nana Patekar of harassing her on the sets of *Horn OK Please* back in 2008. There were videos of her walking out of the set and being hurled abuses at by an aggressive journalist being circulated on the Internet. With her allegations, the #MeToo movement had finally arrived in India, a year after Hollywood's leading ladies spoke up against Harvey Weinstein's abuse. Although it wasn't her intention, Dutta's disclosure had encouraged others in the industry to name men who had harassed and abused them. Vinta Nanda talked about how Alok Nath — India's *sanskaari babu* (the forever patriarch) — had allegedly raped her. Sajid Khan was called out by Sona Mohapatra, Saloni Chopra, and entertainment journalist Karishma Upadhyay. Anu Malik, Vikas Bahl, Piyush Mishra, among others were called out for violating the boundaries of their female colleagues. The film industry's status quo was being challenged as the silence around its biggest open secret finally broke.

Soon enough, the #MeToo movement found its voice among women in the media, spearheaded by journalist Sandhya Menon. Many other women opened up — with rage and urgency, from the stories that had been bubbling inside for years — about just how widespread sexual harassment and misconduct is in the industry. M.J. Akbar, one of the most distinguished editors in the country, and a government official, was accused by not one, but several women. These women stood in solidarity and shared the harrowing details of his predatory misconduct. Excel sheets with names of perpetrators were generously circulated so other women could be informed of whom to be wary of and add their own offenders.

That morning in October, the WhatsApp messages that kept my phone active all day were triggered by women taking to social media platforms like Facebook and Twitter to share their own #MeToo stories. One woman had accused a young man my friends and I knew, of raping her. He was a 'cool' Delhi guy — a photographer; friendly, funny, well-educated, and well-travelled — I choose not to name since the allegations weren't taken forward legally. My friends and I had met and hung out with him on several occasions — on our girls' night outs, Sunday brunches, house parties thrown by mutual friends. One of us had also gone on a date with him.

We were shocked that he had been outed because we felt safe around him! With his half-German ancestry, a younger sister he doted on, dreadlocked hair and polite mannerisms, he was someone we could count on for getting us out of a bad date or chaperoning us back home if we got too drunk. He was that 'woke' guy who didn't display any outwardly signs of stereotypical machismo. That one account alone made us question all the metrics we used to identify a guy as safe or progressive enough to date.

But, that account, and that name, was just the beginning.

Every hour or so, I would get on yet another harried call, type fervently in yet another WhatsApp chat, because yet another person — man — we knew and had hung out with more than once, had been called out. It was a traumatic day, which ended with a sleepless night for me and my friends in Delhi, Jaipur, Bengaluru, Mumbai, Sweden.

The day was spent checking on each other. 'How are you holding up?' we inquired, as if we had lost someone dear. We had, in a way. With so many men we'd had crushes on, some we'd flirted with, others we'd gone home with, now accused of violating a woman's boundaries, how were we to ever trust another man again?

Most importantly, we had lost the belief that sexual harassment was an oddity that happened at the thinning of a bell curve; that we, with our yet unspoken #MeToo stories were among the unlucky 2 per cent of society. Ha! Far from it! The barrage of stories left us feeling that 100 per cent of women had been harassed at some point; that there wasn't a woman out there who didn't have a #MeToo story! We were grieving, and only we could understand each other's anguish.

#METOO BEYOND THE WORKPLACE

Once the initial burst of sadness, anger and shock had subsided, we started talking about the accounts of sexual harassment and abuse we already knew of, many even before the hashtag came about. We kept some accounts to ourselves because we didn't want to bother each other with dark and depressing stuff. Many accounts were those of people we knew — friends, neighbours, relatives, colleagues — and also strangers whose conversations we eavesdropped on in crowded places. There were more accounts we knew of personally than the ones we had read online. And to think that the sheer number of stories that were accompanied by the hashtag has left the world stunned!

The movement has only scratched the surface. It doesn't have space for the #MeToo stories of women who can't afford to out their bosses or colleagues because they risk losing their jobs and future employment; those who are forced to stay in touch with their abuser because the latter is a family member; those in rural India who don't have access to internet; those who face ongoing abuse; those who are still too emotionally pained to talk about what happened to them; those who have been shamed and made to believe that their abuse was somehow their own fault; and finally, those who lost their lives to their #MeToo stories in a horrid combination of sexual assault and murder. And then there are women like me and some of my friends, who simply don't want to share their personal stories on public forums for our own reasons, yet comfort and support each other in private spaces.

#MeToo is about all these stories. All these women, and men. All the men, and women, behind these horrendous acts. Perhaps that's where the grief came from: the heartbreaking reality that the brave women who came out with their stories of abuse were simply a minority.

#MeToo started as a movement to call out sexual harassment at the workplace. The root of the problem it hoped to address is that workplaces are often hostile places for women, and this is detrimental to gender equality and women empowerment because financial independence is key to this. Many women, because of harassment at the workplace either quit jobs they could thrive at or quit working altogether.

But as the movement came into its own, it became clear that the narratives of sexual harassment went far beyond the workplace. #MeToo was a gash on the silence around sexual violence against women that refused to heal. It became bigger and bigger, and bled into corners that weren't in offices.

The stories that came pouring out ranged from being groped in a busy metro to being sexually forced by a partner and everything in between. If women from all walks of life were victims of sexual abuse at the hands of men, it meant that men from all walks of life were potential perpetrators of sexual abuse. This, in turn, means that men can no longer say, 'Well, I'm not a CEO. I don't have that kind of ego. I *can* take no for an answer.' There were no excuses. There were no patterns. There was no profile of an offender that one could draw up.

For a woman, it meant that any man she crosses paths with — in an office or on a dating app — could potentially, at some point, harass or abuse her.

BUT WHAT DID #METOO DO TO MEN?

It was Diwali a month after #MeToo broke in India. The festival of lights is celebrated with unmatched fervour in Delhi. Diwali parties start ten days to two weeks prior, and friends often check with each other to ensure there are no clashes on their calendars. The last thing you want during Diwali season is throwing a party on a date people have already saved for another party! Every year, a dear friend throws a Diwali bash to which she invites all her colleagues, friends and acquaintances. Her annual party is not one to miss because it's that rare event when you get to meet people outside of your clique.

Diwali is also that time of the year that marks the beginning of a busy festive and wedding season. People are in a cheerful mood, all set to dress up and drink up. My friend's party in particular has been home to casual flirtations, no strings attached (NSA) hook ups and people falling in love. There's always been lust and love in the air here.

Not in 2018 though. That year, the women huddled together, stopping at the third drink, and the men kept their eyes down, their hands tightly clutching their glasses. Only couples or close friends of the opposite sex were seen together. There was no flirting that year. Worst of all, the lust in the air had been replaced by fear.

After having said hello to everyone I knew or remembered from previous parties, I stood next to my then-boyfriend now-husband and his male friend. The three of us had made a triangle, or a safe sacred circle if you will. Guests were pouring in and the terrace was getting crowded. Every time a woman would come in our vicinity, our friend would step an inch closer to us. This happened twice. The third time, his hand brushed against a woman's cascading *dupatta.* He swiftly moved his hand up and stepped another two inches forward. 'This is so stressful, man. Next thing I know, #MeToo!' He didn't smile as he said this.

'You know that's not how #MeToo works, right?' I pointed out.

He brushed his hair back with the same hand that had grazed against the woman's dupatta. 'I don't know.' He sighed. 'Like I don't know what's okay and what's not anymore. Can I, like, offer to get a girl a drink?'

'Umm...yes. Offer her a drink. Push her to have a drink, no. Just ask, and if she says, no, leave her alone. It's simple.'

'No...I think I'm fine. *Karna hi nahi hai mujhe kuchh* (I don't want to do anything). I'm fine single ya.'

Over the next few months, I'd learn that while #MeToo had given words to women's fears, it had instilled new fears in men. With only accusations and no conversation or solutions, many men were now left with unanswered questions. Like: Is it okay to flirt with a stranger at a bar or a party? Do you have to ask every time you want to kiss or get physically intimate with someone? What if she doesn't say no, but she's not into it so much? If she has flirted with me and given me all the signs that she wants something more, am I still supposed to ask her?

In an unprecedented manner, men were forced to look inwards at their collective behaviour towards women. And men, women and everyone else, were beginning to question the many toxic, abusive, restrictive and stereotypical patterns of behaviour, society has always normalized.

NORMALIZING OBJECTIFICATION

When Menon brought the conversation to the news and media industry, what came to light was not only how widespread sexual harassment at the hands of powerful men in the industry is, but also how women are expected to 'toughen up' and deal with it. As if it is a part and parcel of being a journalist or being a working woman. This normalization goes beyond newsrooms and other offices.

We normalize men on the streets who ogle, catcall or touch us by saying 'they come from small cities; they are not used to seeing women out and about like this', or, when we put the onus on the woman to carry pepper sprays and tazers and dress modestly. We normalize adolescent boys objectifying, sexualizing and pushing adolescent girls into acts they aren't comfortable with when we say, 'Their hormones are raging. They'll grow out of it. Boys will be boys.' We normalize partners demanding sex as when they fancy when we say, 'Men are driven by their sex drive.' We normalize male sexual pleasure being prioritized over female sexual pleasure when we accept that sex is done when the man is done. And in doing so, we normalize women simply being receptacles of male sexual desire.

#MeToo, among other things, has lifted the veil from this sexist, toxic culture of objectifying women in myriad ways. It has brought the conversation around gender issues to the masses and shed light on the social attitudes that normalize sexual violence. Men and women alike are, in large numbers, questioning, evaluating, assessing their behaviour, attitudes, biases and gendered ways. We have gone beyond sharing stories and are defining and redefining appropriate sexual boundaries. The movement has also put many of us in a retrospective mode. Women and men are looking back at things they have been through, or done, and are wondering if those were violations of boundaries.

In the wake of the movement, my best friend and I couldn't help but spend hours evaluating our past relationships, flirtations and sexual encounters. We realized that our boundaries were sometimes violated because we didn't know what was acceptable and what wasn't, and this — this ubiquitous lack of understanding of consent among both genders — is yet another important dysfunction that the movement brought to light.

LOVE IN THE TIME OF #METOO

In the weeks following #MeToo, the sheer sight of my boyfriend made me angry. Even though he was empathetic at best, and silent at worst, I projected my disdain for all the men who had been outed onto him. I wondered how other heterosexual couples coped with #MeToo, if at all.

Priyanka Sethi is a resident of New Delhi. In her mid-thirties, she's a mom to a four-year-old boy, and a two-year-old handmade jewellery business. Priyanka used to be a 'party girl', but her new responsibilities as a wife, mom and entrepreneur made her an early-to-bed, early-to-rise kind of person. A year into their marriage, and well before #MeToo, she once walked in on her husband groping a female colleague at an office party. 'There was so much drama after that. That woman cried and begged. She said she didn't want it.

Told me Suraj forced himself on her. Obviously, I was livid at the time. But I didn't believe her, and I forgave him.'

She didn't make eye contact with me while she talked about this. With her gaze moving from her coffee cup to the view outside her balcony, she told me how after #MeToo, she could no longer pretend that her husband was a 'clean man'.

'So what did you do then?' She was still with her husband, so I wondered if she swallowed the bitter pill, silently hoping the woman wouldn't name him publicly.

'I told him to apologize to her.'

'Did he?'

For the first time that afternoon, she looked straight at me and smiled. 'Of course not!' She sighed. 'He said I was being unreasonable.' Her husband is an amicable man. He takes centerstage at parties with his entertaining stories and quick wit and is inaccessible in the manner that many men in suits and ties are. I asked Priyanka if I could speak to him. Priyanka already knew his answer and invited me to brunch the following Sunday. At brunch, she excused herself on the pretext of checking on their son.

Alone with a man I already disliked, I wasted no time and got straight to business. I told him I was working on a book and began to give him more context. 'Yes, I know,' he cut me off. Classic toxic male behaviour. 'Priyanka told me you wanted to talk to me about Harshita.'

I asked him what happened that night. 'Nothing "happened". It was a party, everyone was having fun, and I got a bit too drunk. Don't you ever get a little wild after drinking too much?' he asked me.

'Do you?' I throw his question back at him.

'I mean, it happens. Sometimes when you're drunk you don't know what you're doing. I was just having fun. I think Harshita is attractive. I didn't want to hurt her.'

I asked him his thoughts on #MeToo. 'I think it's a bit of an exaggeration. Some of these women sound like they are overreacting.'

Swarnima Narayan's story echoed Suraj's banishment of women's #MeToo stories. Over the phone one Sunday afternoon, she told me that she broke up with her ex-boyfriend because of his dismissal of the narratives that had come up, including her own. 'So, conversation would start with some Tweet or Facebook post that someone else posted. And I'd start telling him that something similar happened to me. But he would find a way to make it about my behaviour. Why did I drink so much? Or why didn't I find another way of getting home?'

Almost three years later, Swarnima is in a relationship with another man, also in his mid-twenties, like her and her ex-boyfriend. 'With him, things are different. He wants to understand what happened, what I went through as opposed to what I did. He asks me pertinent questions about those incidents.'

Three years later, the initial shock of #MeToo which was met with a knee-jerk reaction of #NotAllMen seems to have withered, for both men and women. I ask Swarnima if talking about consent and sexual boundaries with a partner is easier after #MeToo. 'It's less awkward,' she says. 'But that is not to say that women, and men, have stopped giving in to situations they aren't comfortable with.'

BUT AFTER ALL, IT IS A MAN'S WORLD

Romantic relationships are changing rapidly for many reasons — women focusing more on their careers and being less willing to compromise financial independence, the advent of online dating apps, revised laws that now recognize women's issues and changing gender norms. #MeToo has added another aspect to this cultural overhaul. But we have just begun to loosen the grip of patriarchy in society. We have a long way to go before we can learn to conduct our relationships free of generations of conditioning of rigid gender roles.

There is no law in India that forbids women from working. In fact, there are laws that protect women from workplace sexual harassment, and laws for equal renumeration.[1]

Yet, in many parts of the country, families — or male partners — don't support working women. Or when they 'allow' the women in their families to hold down jobs, it often comes with many restrictions. The issue seems to be prevalent across all socio-economic classes. And here's something interesting. While the gender gap in education in India is fast closing,[2] only 3.7 per cent of chief executive officers (CEOs) and managing

[1] The Prohibition of Sexual Harassment of Women at Workplace Act, 2013; The Equal Renumeration Act, 1976

[2] Shukla, Amandeep, 'Education Ministry's AISHE Report Shows More Female Students Pursuing Higher Education', *India Today*, 10 June 2021. Web Desk, *India Today*, '46 Per Cent of Students in India are Women', *India Today*, 27 October 2016

directors (MDs) in NSE-listed companies are women.[1] Women's participation in the labour force has been on a steady decline, and as of 2019, only about 20 per cent of the labour force in India is female.[2]

Meanwhile, a twenty-six-year-old friend based in Mumbai broke up with her boyfriend of three years because he wasn't comfortable with her new job that required late hours. They would end up fighting about her coming home late from work, and he wouldn't understand that for someone just starting to work in a media house, this is the norm.

'Was he insecure?' I ask her.

'No, I don't think so. He just didn't think it was safe for me to be at the office or out on shoots at odd hours. He can't move here [from Bengaluru], so he doesn't see that it's okay. I'm safe.'

She dumped him instead of her job, but how many women can make that choice?

In many urban, educated families, a woman pursuing her ambition is accepted, and even lauded, until she gets married and has a child. Then, her long hours and stretched meetings become a cause to judge her as a wife or a mother. Few men, if any at all, are asked, 'How are you managing with the kids?' while they are in a work meeting. If they are making enough money to give their child a good lifestyle, all is forgiven.

A former colleague from an affluent Delhi family told me of his female cousin who was having a hard time because her father had been pressuring her to

[1] Dhillon, Chitvan Singh and Singh, Navdeep, 'Disappearing Through The Cracks', *The Telegraph Online*, 7 April, 2020

[2] ILOSTAT Database, International Labour Organization, 'Labor Force Participation Rate, Female', *The World Bank*, 15 June, 2021

change her job. The reason? She was earning more than a potential suitor that she and her family liked, and it seemed, to her father, that the young man was uncomfortable with the fact that his potential wife drew a heftier pay cheque than him. I ask my colleague what he thinks about it. He's in his late twenties at the time of this conversation. 'Obviously, you can't change the way the older generation thinks. They [her family] just want her to be happy, so I understand. It's okay to compromise, I feel. Anyway, when she has a kid, she'll have to work less.'

My heart sinks as I listen to these words come out of a young man's mouth. How long will it take for society to treat a woman's career as central to her identity in the same way a man's career is?

Through the course of working on the book, I came across several couples — and men, specifically — for whom the female partner's career is, indeed, central to her identity. In fact, for some men I spoke to, a financially independent partner is a source of support and relief. But even within well-educated, well-traveled and well-aware circles this is not yet the norm.

An increasing number of women now refuse to put their careers on the back burner to suit the social order. Not only are women delaying marriage, many are also delaying motherhood. Neharika Kapoor (name changed) is a marketing consultant in Mumbai. I met her on Leap Club, an up-and-coming networking app for working women. We took our conversation to Zoom where she told me that several of her female colleagues have chosen to freeze their eggs either because they haven't met the right guy or because they don't want to disrupt their career trajectory. Later, I mentioned this to a friend in New Delhi who told me that two of his closest friends, both in their late thirties, had also recently frozen their eggs for similar reasons. Women also no longer need men for financial support. They need men for an emotional connection, sexual compatibility, companionship, friendship and support, trust and love. Men, on the other hand, don't yet seem to be fully accustomed to this idea.

Ayush Chandra, a clinical psychologist practicing in New Delhi, tells me, 'We have working women now, but we still have the glass ceiling. Our generation has grown up seeing stereotypical gender roles play out in the family. Most men in their twenties and thirties now have mothers who were homemakers and are happy as homemakers. This is the role we have grown up seeing the women in, so it will take time to change.'

While women are striving for a balance between pursuing their professional and personal goals, men still bear the burden of becoming breadwinners for the family — this, according to social diktat, is the ideal man; one who can bank enough rupees to feed and shelter several people. Even if a man finds a partner who earns enough to financially support the family, his own sense of worth is still derived from how much money he brings into the household. This is just one of the many banes of patriarchy bestowed upon men.

Rajat Mittal is a techie by training who gave up his cushy job in IT to pursue a career in the creative field. He co-founded the popular series Menstrupedia. When Rajat became a father to a young boy, he didn't want to pass on this burden of being the 'provider' to his son. Wanting to break the chain, he published a series of essays called 'Boyish' in which he showcased men thriving in non-masculine careers. Rajat and I caught up to talk about 'Boyish'. In the process, I learnt that a man's identity is deeply intertwined with his professional life. Rajat tells me, 'Men have inherited or absorbed certain principles — I have to be a stoic personality, always focus on wealth and social status, and internalizing this will satisfy my provider status. We never grew up seeing ourselves as other than our jobs, or outside of our financial or social status. It's hard for [most] millennial men to have a sense of identity if you strip [them off] their job or financial status. Men need to cultivate their identity outside of that tunnel vision.'

There's a ray of hope. Jaiwin Joy is a twenty-two-year-old from the Pink City. When he talks about his girlfriend, his cheeks turn a shade of pink. Smitten as he is with his girlfriend of two years, he can't keep himself from smiling. Proudly, he tells me, 'She wants to be a military nurse.' I ask him what that would mean for their future (we've already discussed their marriage plans by now), half expecting him to say she'll have to give up her dreams. '*Voh jahan jaayegi, saath mein hi jaoonga uske* (I'll go wherever she gets posted). We just want to be together.' A *fauji* husband in the making.

What It Means to Be a Man

'One, two, three... these Russian hookers came to our room and stood in a line.'

—Pranav, thirty-one

I'M AT A FAMILY lunch. I scan the room for someone who'd make me the least uncomfortable and gravitate towards a cousin and her husband who are ten and thirteen years my senior respectively. They have a seventeen-year-old daughter who, from the looks of it, is being raised with progressive values. By this, I mean, she's a class topper. Every year, she travels unchaperoned by parents to study abroad for a semester. Her parents and grandparents boast about her academic achievements, and she seems to be on the path of joining the 3.7 per cent female top brass. I want to hang out with her parents.

Ten minutes in, I start telling them that I'm working on a book about gender and romance. I keep it generic because, at the time of this conversation, the book was still in its nascent stage. 'The problem is,' my cousin's husband begins, 'women nowadays want to be like men they want to hold jobs, drink, smoke, use abusive language...but they can't. They can't ever be like men, and now they are becoming less and less like women. They are losing their worth.'

I am shocked at the contradiction between his emphasis on his daughter's education, and his belief that women wanting to work is an overstep. Then, I think about the many educated women out there who gave up their professional aspirations for domestic duties. For many people in our country, the definition of womanhood lies in her being domestic and free of vice. And the definition of manhood means to have a job, drink, smoke and use abusive language. This is an apt example of what toxic masculinity is — to box men as money-making machines with reckless vices and no regard for their health, and of course, bad manners.

Where does this leave men who find joy in cooking and having leisurely conversations with their loved ones, men who find bliss in being fathers, men who choose not to be a part of boys' clubs where they only drink, smoke and talk about their bank balances and the big deals they cracked, men who are polite? Well, with their partners and families, away from the boys' club.

Pranav and Dhruv went to college together. They were two among a group of five boys who were extremely close. During the three years they spent at Delhi University (DU), they had most of their meals together, spent many drunk nights on the paying guest (PG) terrace where three of the five lived, learnt how to cook, made and lost girlfriends, travelled to McLeod Ganj and Goa several times, and swore to be friends forever. After graduation, higher education and jobs took three of them to different cities, leaving Pranav and Dhruv behind in Delhi. The five of them stayed in touch. They would get together at least twice a year. Then they fell in love. Now in their thirties, all of them are married. Two have kids.

Dhruv is one of the two fathers in the group. When his wife started showing, Dhruv began visiting the neon-lined streets of Mahipalpur in Delhi — a busy marketplace by day and a prostitution hub by night.

At Pranav's house, he tells me why he isn't in touch with the group anymore. We are six months into the pandemic, and Pranav and his wife have not stepped out of the house yet. I'm their third visitor in six months. Pranav makes chai for us as he tells me about Dhruv, while his wife gets mugs and snacks in place.

'You know he took me there one night. I was shocked! He just said, "*Chal baahar chalte aaj* (Let's go out)." And he took me to this shady hotel. He said let's get a room and drink *araam se.* So we ordered a bottle, and started with our drinks. Then...' He pauses and raises both his eyebrows. His jaw drops, as if he's visualizing what he's about to tell me next. Behind him, his wife shakes her head and rolls her eyes. 'One, two, three… these Russian hookers came to our room and stood in a line. I was shocked. I didn't even know this happens in Delhi! I just couldn't believe it.'

Pranav texted his wife and asked her to call and feign an emergency so he could get out of the seedy hotel. 'That's the only time he's ever done something like that. Otherwise, he's always the last to leave a place.'

That night marked the beginning of the unraveling of 'toxic masculinity' in the group. The next time the five of them were back together in Delhi, Dhruv suggested the boys make a visit to Mahipalpur, while the wives could have a girls' night. When Pranav protested, he was made fun of.

'Yaar, don't you get bored of the same routine with the wife?'

'Ha ha. You're a sissy!'

'The wife keeps you on a tight leash.'

We, as a society, can't handle men who show a sensitive side. Take a moment to consider how people react when a man cries as opposed to when a woman does the same. Both in reel life and real life, we don't see enough healthy representations of a man expressing sadness. In pop culture, a man crying is often the butt of jokes. When a woman sheds a tear or two, it is no big deal. It's just another day, another mood, another low moment that will pass. A low moment that has no real gravity and warrants no real reaction. It is considered 'normal' for women to cry, encouraged even. It doesn't surprise or shock us, and it certainly doesn't catch us off guard. But when a man cries, even the most progressive among us are guilty of having at least a moment where we don't know how to respond to this display of vulnerability. We may freeze in panic, as if a man's tears are almost a threat to the delicate balance of human interaction. We may go overboard trying to comfort him, as if he is not capable of comforting himself. We may ignore the tears altogether because we feel that they are a manipulation tactic and aren't in fact an expression of sadness. Or we may find ourselves overwhelmed by the sadness hidden in the tears because a man must be terribly broken to come to this point of a meltdown. Tears are considered a meltdown for a man, and an everyday occurrence for a woman.

Everybody pays a price for gender stereotypes. When women are expected to be submissive and cooperative, any act of self-preservation is immediately regarded as selfish. But men, too, pay a price for the prescription of masculinity. Or, what has come to be known as 'toxic masculinity'.

UNDERSTANDING TOXIC MASCULINITY

Patriarchal customs and values have armed men with generous amounts of 'toxic masculinity' — a deeply misunderstood term we didn't have until recently. I have heard the term toxic masculinity being used in various contexts:

A pushy date who doesn't get the hint that a woman is not interested.

A boyfriend who's been going on too many boys' nights lately.

Laughing at — or worse, cracking — inarguably misogynistic jokes.

A guy who's dating multiple women at the same time and lying to each one of them. All these contexts bring up the term toxic masculinity.

But when it comes to defining toxic masculinity, most people fall short. I did, too, until I learnt that toxic masculinity is not synonymous with bad behaviour. Bad behaviour is merely a symptom of toxic masculinity. And until we understand and address the root cause, the symptoms will simply keep evolving.

To understand toxic masculinity — a term that invokes many emotions — we must first understand masculinity. Masculinity is a socially constructed set of behaviours, attributes, attitudes and traits that are associated with being male. It is important to note that the male sex in itself is not necessarily masculine. Rather, the latter is simply how the society expects the male sex to be.

Maleness and femaleness are biological and are defined based on one's hormones and genitalia. However, masculine and feminine are social and cultural, and defined on the basis of one's behaviour and mannerisms.

MASCULINE	*FEMININE*
Strong	Emotional
Ruthless	Submissive
Rational	Artistic
Aggressive	Forgiving
Fearless	Compassionate
Outgoing	Nurturing
Focused	Kind
Hard-working	Social
Perseverant	Understanding
Impatient	Patient
Un-emotional	Gullible

The table above (not exhaustive) highlights that masculinity is not all negative or 'toxic'. In fact, there are some masculine traits that are aspirational for all. The same can be said for feminine traits. However, years of gendered socialization has crystallized these and more such polarized personality traits at the cost of the social, interpersonal and mental health of both genders.

Toxic masculinity is the dark side of masculinity — putting on a brave front even when one may be terrified, working relentlessly to the point of complete exhaustion, suppressing one's emotions until they explode in the form of mental or physical illness or substance abuse, high risk-taking behaviours in the name of 'being a man'. These are mere examples, and not a definition. What is, however, indubitable is that toxic masculinity harms women, children and men themselves. Because of this expectation to 'man up', men are more susceptible to depression, anxiety and other mental illnesses; are less likely to seek help[3]; more likely to engage in risky sexual practices like not using condoms;[4] and less likely to seek healthcare when needed;[5] more likely to abuse drugs and binge-drink alcohol.

There are several limitations, biases and stereotypes that men face thanks to patriarchy. Here are some examples:

They can't express their emotions freely:
A man crying is an anomaly, not because men willingly and happily suppress emotions, but because they are expected to do so by society's norms. It is a part of 'being a man'. Boys don't cry, etc. Should a man decide to break down this wall and allow himself to

---

[3] M.J. Sharpe, P.P. Heppner, 'Gender Role, Gender-role Conflict, and Psychological Wellbeing in Men', *Journal Of Counselling Psychology*, 1991

[4] M.C. Santana, A Raj, M.R. Decker, A. La Marche, J.G. Silverman, 'Masculine Gender Roles Associated with Increased Sexual Risk and Intimate Partner Violence Perpetration Among Young Adult Men', National Center for Biotechnology Information, 2006

[5] P. J. Fleming, J. G. L. Lee, S.L. Dworkin, '"Real Men Don't": Constructions of Masculinity and Inadvertent Harm in Public Health Interventions', *American Journal of Public Health*, 2014

be emotionally expressive — whether that's in love, sadness, exhaustion, fear — he is considered to be something extraordinary.

Repeatedly, I asked men what they do when they are feeling low. Their answers can be summed up in one word: escape. This escape comes in many forms, and not one involves verbal or creative expression of emotions. They range from playing video games to exercising, learning about investments and stocks, drinking with guy friends.

Men face immense pressure to earn enough money to support a family:

A stay-at-home husband or dad is a new concept, one that is not yet fully accepted by any strata of society (except for matrilineal societies where this is the norm). But it's not simply about being a working father or stay-at-home father. Men are expected to take up high paying jobs. Earning money is more important than their career interests, work-life balance and mental health, regardless of his partner's financial status.

While working women have more flexibility in that they can take a break for marriage or motherhood, men are expected to work all their lives. Rajat points out: 'What strikes me is that being a provider has to be continuous for men. From the time you start working — twenty-two or around that — it's just nonstop. From that point on, up until your sixties and seventies. That's like fifty-odd non-stop years of shouldering that expectation. You can't even take a break! Can an adult man in his thirties and forties say, hey I'm just going to take five years off and cultivate my love for writing or art, and then get back to doing what I'm doing? Even that is a foreign concept!'

A man's sense of worth as a partner, too, is often tied with how well he can provide. Karthik is a thirty-five-year-old professor teaching in a tier two city. His wife is currently pursuing her PhD at Indian Institute of Technology (IIT) Delhi. While telling me about how his torrid marriage finally began healing, he says, 'It happened when I sorted out my finances. I gave my wife all my investment details, bank account information and told her it's all hers. She has the control.' It sounded like his worth as a husband was tied to how well he can provide. I asked him if his wife had any plans to work in the future. 'Yes yes. When she finishes her PhD, she will earn four to five times more than me.' He then puts on his professor hat (I have learnt that intellectualization is a defence mechanism men often resort to) and tells me how marriage evolved because of a need for proprietorship — owning land, children, women. I steer the conversation back to him and his marriage. 'I just wanted to show my wife that she is taken care of, I will take care of her. I am not giving my money to someone else.'

Even for Jaiwin, the fauji husband in the making, it is important that he is on a steady career path before they even think of marriage. For men in their twenties though, it seems the rules are more or less the same for everyone: he wants to have a steady flow of income, and he wants the same for his girlfriend; for her to settle down in her career before she settles down in a marriage.

A man's virility is seen as a measure of his worth

The idea that a man's worth is tied with his sexuality comes up in many different ways. We call a man who has many lovers a 'stud'. We assume that a man is always ready for sex, or that all male sexuality operates as separate from emotion or mental well being.

Pradyum, thirty-seven, pointed out to me that most content — whether it's articles or movies — assumes that men always enjoy sex. He tells me, 'A lot still remains unsaid due to social stigma or preconceived notions.' I ask him what these unsaid things are. With the disclaimer that he's no expert, he tells me that work pressure and family stress can hamper desire; that men also need to feel appreciated and, like women, men also have the need to feel loved.

But male sexuality is a wide spectrum, and on the other end lies *bandibaazi*. Sounds like a sport, doesn't it? As I learnt, *bandibaazi* means a pick-up game. So yes, it is like a sport for some men. When a man wins at this game, the woman becomes his trophy — one he can flaunt.

Social norms also excuse men of a lot of things that are expected of women. Take any domestic chore for instance. Keeping the house in order, cooking and maintaining harmony in the family is a woman's job. Men are not expected to be concerned with such domestic matters. Unlike women, men are not pressured to learn how to cook or to keep up with the laundry schedule or haggle with domestic help. But in the modern society, where an increasing number of men and women are choosing to live alone or with their partners, without parental support, and with both sexes taking up jobs with long hours, these have become basic survival skills that every individual needs to be equipped with. Men not knowing the fundamentals of running a household is a common phenomenon in our country — our men are infamous for not knowing how to cook much beyond boiling an egg or whipping up some Maggi. But this doesn't work for the young, urban Indian trying to make a career as well as a home. The difference between men and women though is that while most women fly from the nest equipped with some basic survival skills like cooking, grocery shopping and budgeting, men have to learn on their own.

One after another, men told me they learnt how to cook and keep the house clean and organized only when they moved out of their parents' home and started living on their own or with their partner. In other words, they stepped up when there was no other choice.

I ask them if they wish they'd been taught these skills before. Twenty-nine-year-old Ankur tells me he ended up spending a ton of money ordering in food when he first started living alone. He didn't know how to cook 'even the basic dishes like rice, chicken and vegetables'. He also tells me that he envies the women in his life because they are better at handling money. 'But I think it's because I'm bad at math,' he jokes. It's not.

Forty-year-old Sourav is hands-on and house-proud. He and his wife divide chores like cooking and cleaning, and he likes to have things in order. But, as he tells me, 'this was an evolution'. Back at his parental home, where there were three men and one woman, all domestic responsibilities were supervised by his mother. When

I ask him if men should be taught domestic skills from boyhood, he agrees without blinking. 'Everyone, regardless of their gender, should be taught basic skills.'

For Dev it was somewhere in the middle. He could cook a meal for himself but didn't know other skills like running the washing machine or ironing clothes. He learnt that from his wife. The young couple take pride in their home and share responsibilities. 'If you share house work and make a home together, it gives the couple an ever evolving project, which you both learn from. It keeps you occupied and happy.'

When Dev and his wife bought their first house together, it was he who set it up. His wife was handling a project which left her with no time or energy for home. That left him to his devices. He arranged the furniture around the house, set up the kitchen and the bar. 'I enjoyed the process,' he tells me. 'And my wife even bragged about it to everyone. But later she changed everything around. I had all the furniture pointed to the TV or the bar. Something I learnt is a mistake later that year.'

Many men take pride in domestic work, in setting up and running a home, but most have a lot to learn. In most cases, it's either a woman or a diminishing bank balance that compels men to get a grip on handling the home and other basics.

I'm at a birthday party hosted by four men in their twenties who live together. Among the fifteen or so guests, only four, including me, are women. There's place to sit, booze to drink and food to eat. But the chips are served straight from the packet, the fresh paper cups are still in the cellophane wrapper and are strewn on the floor next to the table. Dinner is served on paper plates and we're running short on tissues. It's chaotic but the boys hosting the party are thrilled that everyone they invited showed up!

Not all masculinity is toxic but like the dirty toilet at this bachelors' pad, the ineptitude of men as a result of gendered socialization prevents women from completely letting their guard down. Where there's always something to fix or teach, there's little room left for abandon.

Men and Mental Health

'I liked being angry. I wanted to hate the world, be angry, so I didn't have to be sad'

— Dhairya, thirty-four

'Why are you pursuing psychology? It's a female-centric field. Girls are more interested in emotions, and they can understand it better,' Ayush Chandra, whom you met in chapter one, was often told when he decided to study psychology.

Mental health — a nascent field in our country — is dominated by women. The very word 'counsellor' sparks the image of a woman wearing a cotton saree and thick-rimmed glasses, her hair tied in a bun and a gentle look on her face. And sitting across this feminine figure, one envisions another woman. The idea that mental health is for women manifests on both sides — women offer mental health services and women seek mental health services.

Chandra runs a private practice with his fiancée. They've been able to attract young men to their clinic. But the men who come for therapy or counselling tend to open up more to Chandra than his fiancée. 'They feel more comfortable talking to me. They feel they can be more open about certain things.'

So, perhaps it is a vicious cycle that begins when we tell young boys they shouldn't study 'softer' subjects like psychology or sociology. We deter them from entering these professions, and when adult males are in need of mental health services, they don't see themselves represented among the professionals. While experiences change us and encourage us to evolve, childhood experiences and the subtle messages we receive, leave a mark on us. Mental health care is seen as something for the weak-hearted. As therapist Anaya Sethi mentions in an interview with *Times of India*, 'A person who seeks therapy is considered weak and mentally unstable, and people often think there's something wrong with them.'[1] Even today, despite the varsity of Google at everyone's fingertips, depression is seen as something that affects only the feeble. Women, not men. Year after year, the NCBR data shows that more men than women commit suicide.[2] This isn't exclusive to India. The high suicide rate among men is a global phenomenon.[3] According to Rory O'Connor, President of the International Academy of Suicide Research at University of Glasgow, the high suicide rate among men has to do with what he calls 'social perfectionism'.[4]

---

[1] Deb, Rishabh, 'Why Are We Still So Hesitant About Seeking Therapy?', *Times Of India*, 22 July, 2020

[2] National Crime Records Bureau, 'Accidental Deaths and Suicides in India', 2019

[3] Rathi, Akshat, 'Men Are Committing Suicide More Than Women Everywhere In The World. Why?,' *Quartz India*, 13 May, 2015

[4] Storr, Will, 'The Male Suicides: How Social Perfectionism Kills,' *Mosaic Science*, 11 May, 2015

When men can't fit into the socially prescribed ideal of what it means to be a man, they experience shame and guilt, which ultimately leads them to decide their life is not worth living.

Regardless of the reasons behind suicide, we turn a blind eye to mental health issues among men. The desperation of this denial came to surface when the news of Sushant Singh Rajput's death broke. Before we could wrap our heads around that the fact that the country's budding heartthrob was gone, #whokilledssr began trending on Twitter. There was a big furore over the alleged murder of the actor even before his last rites were carried out. In the media trial, the verdict was already out — Rajput couldn't possibly have killed himself. When the hope of finding evidence that could prove he was murdered dwindled, many began blaming the actress Rhea Chakraborty. The narrative went from 'he couldn't have killed himself' to 'if he killed himself, it was because this woman he loved drove him to it'. On Twitter, it was decided, suicide was not something a man like him would ever commit.

The sentiment echoed in living rooms too. Here's a scene from a casual soirée a few weeks after Rajput's death:

Woman 1, thirty: 'Apparently, there's some video circulating that proves it was murder. The cop is saying it.'

Man 1, twenty-nine: 'Has to be. Can't be suicide, man. He was doing so well for himself. Had made a place for himself in the industry.'

Man 2, thirty-one: 'Exactly! Why would he kill himself? It makes no sense.'

Woman 2, twenty-nine: 'But he was depressed they're saying. He was undergoing treatment.'

Man 2: 'It's bullshit. Everybody gets depressed. But suicide is just plain weak. You have to be really weak to kill yourself.'

Woman 1: 'Well, he did struggle a lot in the industry. He might have been having a hard time.'

Man 1: 'Everyone struggles, man. But that doesn't mean you get depressed about it or kill yourself. That's a sign of weakness.'

'A sign of weakness.' This same phrase invokes so much shame among some men who itch to get out of the 'man box'.

Rajput's autopsy report confirmed suicide and ruled out foul play.[5] Yet, even today, #justiceforssr will trend on Twitter every week or so. So strong is our denial that men, too, hurt sometimes.

'BOYS DON'T CRY' IS MORE THAN A TRENDY PUNCHLINE

When I asked men what they thought might be the biggest challenge patriarchy posed to them, almost all of them brought up the diktat that 'boys don't cry'. Some spoke of it in superficial terms, as if regurgitating what they'd seen trending on the Internet. Others shared stories of how they had been shamed and bullied for being 'sensitive'. Yet others countered this with their definition of masculinity that meant to be 'stoic'.

[5] Web Desk, 'Sushant Singh Rajput's Final Autopsy Report Confirms Suicide; Rules Out Foul Play', *The Week*, 24 June, 2020

But 'boys don't cry' isn't just a punchline for ads and campaigns. When I asked Ayush about this, he said, 'Toxic masculinity begins with this idea that boys don't cry.' He goes on to tell me about alexithymia. 'These days, we talk a lot about this idea. But it's actually true. Telling young boys not to cry, not to be weak, actually makes them unable to feel and express their emotions.'

Coined by Ronald F. Levant of Nova Southeastern University, Normative Male Alexithymia (NMA) refers to a man's inability to put emotions into words.[6] According to the proponents of NMA, this stunting of emotional expression is a result of gender-stereotypical upbringing and socialization. Research shows that male toddlers are more emotionally sensitive and expressive than female toddlers.[7]

However, by adolescence, boys become *less* expressive than girls. This is attributed to parenting styles which expose girl children to a wider range of emotions and experiences while discouraging boys from showing so-called 'weaker' emotions.

NMA is a spectrum rather than a list of symptoms or signs.[8] This means that some men are less capable of expressing emotions than others. Where a man lies along the spectrum is directly related to the severity of his rigid and gender-compliant upbringing. So the

---

[6] Levant, Ronald F., Pollack, William S., *A New Psychology of Men* (HarperCollins, United States, 1995), pp. 44, 238–40.

[7] Chaplin, Tara M., and Aldao Amelia, 'Gender Differences In Emotion Expression: A Meta-Analytic Review', *Psychological Bulletin*, 2013

[8] Levant, Ronald F., Allen Philip A, Lien, Mei-Ching, 'Alexithymia In Men: How And When Do Emotional Processing Definiciences Occur?', *Psychology of Men and Masculinity*, July, 2014

harsher the consequences for a young boy showing vulnerability, the less emotionally expressive he will be as a man. The more we deny young boys expressing their emotions, the less emotionally expressive they become. When it comes to nature versus nurture, nurture often has more power than we think.

WHERE DO EMOTIONS GO?

As a student of psychology, I learnt that emotions are like little children asking for attention and care. They start with a whisper, a small gesture. When that doesn't work, they begin to get louder. Some children cry. Others throw tantrums. If children are reprimanded even after that, they may go quiet but their need for attention doesn't disappear. They simply take that need elsewhere.

Emotions work the same way. When reprimanded, they may become silent for a while, but they linger under the surface. Indian men are like pressure cookers. With a tight lid and high flame, their emotions simmer inside until they explode. Chandra tells me he sees this explosion in his male clients. 'If you keep piling up your emotions, after a point, there will be a blast which will destroy your work, friendships, relationships, everything. Mental health is not just something you suffer in silence. It affects your bio-psycho-social needs.'

Bio-psycho-social: biological, psychological, social. These three pillars uphold the structure of life. Each one impacts the other two. When we neglect any one of these three elements of well-being, the other two begin to weaken.

'You become an angry man. Because young boys are told — *aadmi hai toh ladna aana chahiye* (men must be fighters) — this "man up" concept actually messes up manhood. This starts becoming a problem in your twenties or thirties when you want to settle down, have a partner or a serious relationship...that's when you realize you don't even know what it means to be in love.'

This 'angry young man' is a male archetype that has been normalized at the very least, and celebrated at worst, in its many forms. From Amitabh Bachchan's reel and real-life portrayal to Virat Kohli's volatile temper, we almost expect men to be short-fused and unable to control their anger.

In many cases, when a man is indeed angry most people walk on eggshells around him so as to not provoke him. One doesn't want to be the reason why a short-tempered man has lost his cool. Parents, partners, siblings and even friends, tend to deal with this by avoiding provocation, and ignoring anger bursts, waiting for them to pass. Rarely do we pause and wonder if it's a problem that requires psychological intervention. This is a sign of how we have normalized and accepted that men are angry, when in fact, as Chandra points out, the anger is a result of years of conditioning young boys to not show any emotion.

So, where do emotions go when we tell young boys not to cry?

They get bottled up. Sometimes the lid is so tightly fastened that you can't open it no matter how hard you try. At other times, so much is stuffed inside the bottle that it explodes and destroys everything in its wake. 'Emotions don't go anywhere,' says Chandra.

'Eventually, you reach a point of frustration and resentment, and when that happens, you pick fights with everyone around you. Or you develop maladaptive behaviours like drug addiction. In some cases, it leads to anxiety or depression. It takes a hit on your immune system. And even obesity can be caused by unresolved emotions. If you notice, some people eat very little but are not able to lose weight. That happens when you mindlessly eat high calorie foods because of stress, which can be caused by unresolved emotions.'

One word that came up often in my conversations about masculinity was 'stoic'. Men from all walks of life, and at different stages of life — between college and fatherhood — would gravitate to this idea of being 'stoic' while speaking about different facets of masculinity. Most men seem to regard the emotional equanimity of a stoic as an ideal to strive for, oblivious to how it impacts them or those around them.

'To be a man means to not be easily swayed. Not get easily bothered by things and do what you need to do. That's what men do. It's just the practical thing to do. You can't sit around and mope. You have to deal with things without letting them affect you,' twenty-seven-year-old Rachit tells me.

I can't wrap my head around this idea of carrying on with your daily life without letting anything bother you. I ask him where he got this idea that men don't get swayed easily. Earlier in the conversation, he had used the word 'stoic' along with a slew of other such 'masculine' adjectives — aggressive, focused, strong. It's important to note here that when speaking of stoicism, men often mean it in the colloquial sense of being emotionally detached and unaffected, rather than methodical examination of problems or questions, with the purpose of arriving at an answer in the process.

'So do men not feel sad?' I ask Rachit, flummoxed and curious.

'It's not that men don't feel sad,' he clarifies. 'We feel sad when it is appropriate. When something has happened, there is an appropriate response to it.'

It's July 2020. Three months into the first wave of COVID-19. In April, Rachit was supposed to move to Singapore to join a burgeoning tech startup. When the lockdown was announced in India, he lost that opportunity. When we spoke, he was unemployed and considering starting his own firm. I ask him how that's been going for him. 'It's been fine, actually. I'm just bored out of my mind and I'm drinking a lot. But it's fine.'

'What's a lot?' I ask.

'Like two to three drinks every night,' he pauses, and then, 'I can't sleep without it.'

WHY WOULD A MAN GO FOR COUNSELLING?

'When it comes to lifestyle-related issues, there are three things I see the most in men,' Ayush tells me when I ask him about the common mental health issues he sees among men. 'Relationship conflict, sexual disorders and addiction,' he says. Most men who seek counselling for these issues are between eighteen and thirty-five years of age.

Substance use is a two-pronged fork. One is the 'coolness' factor. The other is a coping mechanism gone wrong. 'These days, there's a big push to make cannabis legal, and I understand that. But as a clinician I see many people who are addicted to it. You don't even realize when your whole day just becomes about smoking a joint,' Chandra tells me.

As late teenagers and young adults, many of us experiment with substances. Some are able to keep it to just that — *mauj masti* — as Chandra puts it. Fun and frolic. Others, however, don't realize when recreation becomes an addiction. Having said that, data shows that twice as many men than women develop alcohol dependence.[1]

For Dhairya, alcohol became a coping mechanism when his on-again-off-again relationship of two years fell apart. He withdrew from his friends, couldn't sleep, started working long hours and drinking copious amounts. He also gained a lot of weight (remember what Chandra had said about unresolved emotions and weight gain?). Dhairya was a mess and pissed off with the world. 'I liked being angry. I wanted to hate the world, be angry, so I didn't have to be sad,' he tells me. So, he drowned himself in work and beer. But the one thing he didn't do was cry.

'I never cried,' he says.

When I ask him if it was because he was shutting himself off, he corrects me, 'No. I've *never* cried. In my whole life, I've never cried. It's because I was never taught that crying was normal. Growing up, you see all these grown men — my Dad, for me — who are always just level. I never saw my Dad too sad or too happy. He was just okay, always. That's how most men

[1] 'Gender and Women's Mental Health', World Health Organization, 2002

are, and that's what most men see. So, it doesn't occur to you to cry.'

But it occurs to you to take to the bottle? What Dhairya tells me next goes to show how substance use as a coping mechanism is reinforced by social norms.

'You tell a friend you are going through a break up or generally feeling blah, he'll say, "hey, come on, let's go get a drink. You'll feel better or forget about it." And so that becomes normal,' Dhairya explains.

Drink and forget. Except, like emotions, memories don't go away.

Dhairya is able to re-evaluate those years in hindsight because he went to therapy. When he hit rock bottom — overweight, overworked and under-slept — he decided it was enough and he had to get help. He was in the US at the time, where therapy is more accessible and less taboo. So he started seeing a psychologist who, one week at a time, helped him put the pieces back together. He healed himself, and now knows what to watch out for.

I reconnect with him during the second wave of the pandemic.

'I got into a real alcohol problem a few months back because I kept looking at the news, people dying, others ignoring everything. It just felt like the end of humankind.'

I confessed that I was also having a few too many glasses of wine to cope. We share a laugh about our 'fucked up' coping mechanisms, and after acknowledging that it isn't a healthy way to cope, he tells me he paired up with a friend in the UK to stay sober. They are sobriety buddies who check in on each other and help each other steer away from mind-numbing coping mechanisms. Dhairya replaced the bottle with a cricket bat, and sent me pictures of his bandaged hands, calloused and scathed from the sport.

HOW DO MEN HEAL THEMSELVES?

The veil over men's mental health issues is slowly lifting. But even today, very few men will go for therapy or see a mental health professional. This difference in seeking help seems partly to be because of a difference in perception of mental wellbeing. Men don't see mental health professionals because they are less likely to recognize mental health issues in themselves.[2] Those who do, often seek help only when they hit rock bottom. For Dhairya, it was his rocketing alcohol use. For Arunav, it was a professional crisis that was slowly leading him down a rabbit hole of self-doubt and deprecation that led him to see a psychologist. For Ishan, it was the last resort to save his marriage. For most men, the mantra seems to be: You take to the couch when all else fails.

Some examples of coping mechanisms men resort to include video games, exercise, alcohol, sex, and 'upskilling'.

Video games: Rachit, other than his nightly poison, has been spending a lot of time playing video games. It keeps his mind off the professional limbo he's stuck in.

Exercise: Ishan likes to go for a run in the morning and lift three times a week. If he skips his workout, he feels 'on edge'. When conflicts between him and his

[2] Department of Gender And Women's Health, 'Gender and Mental Health', World Health Organisation, 2002

now ex-wife escalate, Ishan goes to the gym to 'blow off steam'.

Alcohol and other substances: Both Dhairya and Rachit took to the bottle to navigate the difficult times. While there is nothing wrong with winding down with a whiskey or a chilled beer, it becomes a problem when alcohol — or any other substance — becomes a substitute for addressing the issue at hand.

Sex: Some men have a tendency to treat sex as a way to release emotional stress and tension. In the next section, I explore this in great detail. A husband wanting to have sex after spending the day caring for a COVID positive family; a grieving grandson in search of a private spot where he could relieve himself. For now, let's suffice to say that sex, for some, can be a balm for loss of control, a tool to distract from sadness, and finally, a show of one's virility and worthiness as a man.

Learning new skills: When Karthik feels down and out, he reads up on stocks and investment. If it's not this, he will sign up for a course on Coursera or Udemy to keep his mind occupied and learn something new along the way.

FINDING THE MIDDLE GROUND

One Sunday afternoon, while I mindlessly switched from one tab on my phone browser to another, checking Twitter and Instagram in between, I came across an article titled, 'I am a sexual abuse survivor. No, I am not a woman'.[3] Without ado, I clicked on it. Sexually abused

[3] Pawar, Lokesh, 'I Am A Sexual Abuse Surviver. No, I'm Not A Woman', *The Print*, 18 April, 2021

by an uncle, NCRB data on child sexual abuse (in 2018, 109 children were abused every day in India), abused from age six to fifteen, some more data…

I scrolled to the bottom of the page to see if the author's social profiles were linked. I felt an urgency to reach out to him. Women are only beginning to talk about sexual abuse and male sexual abuse is still met with outright denial — *ladkon ke saath nahi hota yeh* (it doesn't happen to boys). And here's a man who's published his account in one of the country's leading publications.

Within minutes, Lokesh replied and an hour later, we got on a call. He tells me it took him years to first understand that what happened to him was sexual abuse, and then, another couple of years before he could talk about it. The journey of coming to terms with sexual trauma is often long and arduous as was his. I ask him if he went for therapy at any point. He didn't. To heal, he says, he read about sexual abuse as much as he could for years on end. Educating himself about what he went through helped him heal.

'I want to get deep into things, and I want to understand the what's and the why's of things,' he says. 'So I started looking at that and listening to and reading stories of abuse of mostly women, because there aren't too many of men in the public domain. It took me four years to understand I was abused. I remember watching an episode on *Satyamev Jayate* where Harish Iyer spoke about this, and that was the time I started realizing, "Oh shit! This is it. This is what I've been through!"'

Many men use education as a healing tool. In therapy, this is an important step — to be able to name what has happened. For some people, this is enough. But Chandra cautions against this. 'You have to be careful about two things — one is to make sure that you're reading a reliable source. You will find all kinds of information on the internet, and a lot of it is incorrect. So you must be careful about this. We all have a confirmation bias; we will pay attention to things that validate our beliefs. So when people search for information online, this happens a lot. The other thing you must be careful about is that sometimes reading about something makes it worse. You're not able to handle the information and it makes you more anxious than before. You need to see a clinician if this happens.' He feels passionately about this and is emphatic about the downfall of educating oneself. 'It's good to educate yourself about mental health issues, but it is equally important to get professional help,' he summarizes.

The Male Entitlement Paradox

'She might change her mind if I try hard enough.'
— Varun, twenty-nine

A FEW YEARS AGO, I heard a story about a man in his early twenties who had set himself on fire. It wasn't as part of a protest or a religious rite of passage to eternal moksha. On the eve of Diwali, he drove to a friend's house, rang the doorbell, and when the friend's father opened the door, he self-immolated. The friend in question was a girl he had been pursuing, who, after mulling over his overtures for some time, finally told him she was not interested. The man could not bear the rejection, and decided to self-destruct, but not without first making sure that the woman who had 'put him in this spot' was haunted by it for the rest of her life.

Extreme as this case may be, the dynamic at play here is not uncommon. I was a popular girl in school. But I didn't realize this until much later; well into my twenties in fact, when I had a few run-ins with former schoolmates. One such man was surprised that I remembered him from back in the day. When I asked him why he 'couldn't believe it', he said, 'Well, I didn't think you ever cared about anyone. You were a bit of a snob.' This was not congruent with my experience or my recollection of those glorious school years. As an angsty teenager, I felt quite the opposite. Isolated, in one word. The boys were too keen to go on dates with me for me to establish any sort of a friendship with them. The girls didn't seem to like me because too many boys were interested in me. My reputation preceded me. All sorts of rumours floated around (including that I had gotten pregnant, when I remained a virgin until years after I graduated high school), and I spent most of my time avoiding people. Allegedly though I had many boyfriends in school and was a Regina George avatar from the movie *Mean Girls*, who was well…mean to the girls.

When I was in eleventh grade, a friend found the source of these rumours. It was a guy named Prakhar who had asked me out, and whom, I had turned down. He went around telling everyone that not only had I slept with him, I had also cheated on him. Wait. It doesn't end there. He proceeded to tell whoever cared to listen that *he* dumped me because of my philandering. It's only in hindsight that I realize that was not simply rogue teenage behaviour stemming from raging hormones. This callous tarnishing of a girl's reputation is a sign of a man's inability to take a no.

The seeds of such entitlement are planted early on, Chandra tells me. 'Being told "no" has different connotations for men. Many men think that if they take a no, it means they are weak or submissive. In our patriarchal society, men are made to feel they have dominance, that their needs are supreme. So when a woman turns them down, they are surprised that their needs are not being satisfied. This is so deeply ingrained that sometimes even they don't understand why they get angry.' What we brush off as teenage angst, then, is actually the sprouting of male entitlement.

As I listen to Chandra speak about how childhood experiences shape our personalities, I can't help but think about the epidemic of the '*raja beta* syndrome' as it is called. Doting mothers pander to the needs of their sons, ignoring indiscretions and rude behaviour. When a young boy throws tantrums, some parents brush it off as behaviour that's typical of males. '*Ladkon ko toh gussa aata hi hai* (it's normal for boys to get angry).' When boundaries are not set in childhood, having to learn them in adulthood often invokes anger, disappointment and irritation.

One fine evening, my best friend and I decided to head out for drinks. We didn't have big plans; we were just catching up over a couple of frozen margaritas. While we were waiting for a table, drinks in hands, a young man with a friend in tow, also awaiting a table, accosted us. It had been made clear during the brief conversation what our plans for the evening were — we were here to catch up with each other. Anyway, my friend and I were the first to get a table. A short while after, the gentleman in question came and asked if he and his friend could join us. We politely declined and told him we just wanted to hang out with each other. He left. Another short while later, the waiter brought two bottles of beer to our table. 'It's from that man over there,' he explained when we said we didn't order beer. We sent it back. Another short while later, a pizza was sent to our table. We refused to accept that too. As soon as the waiter disappeared from our sight, the gentleman in question appeared with the said pizza.

'Come on, girls. Have one slice,' he said jovially. By this point, my friend and I were justifiably irked. Not caring for politeness, we asked him to leave us alone. At last, he got the message, and walked away, but not without first telling us that we had been thankless and rude.

This incident took place before #MeToo, back when most women didn't know how to point out this was a problem. #MeToo became a torch that lit up that dark alley of encroached boundaries and verbal assaults. Now we could say: 'No is a no.' But many men didn't take it well. They missed the whole point.

As a retort to #MeToo, came #NotAllMen, and along with that hashtag came to light just how widespread and pernicious male entitlement can be.

'Men can't hit on a woman anymore,' laments twenty-nine-year-old Varun. He gets impatient with this conversation about how women feel the need to be on guard, and why there is a need to hold men accountable. He is of the tribe that thinks #MeToo was blown out of proportion. 'That's not what we're saying,' I tell him. 'All we're saying is when a woman says no, you leave her alone.'

'But, how can they say no without even getting to know a guy?'

'Could be any number of reasons, but that shouldn't matter. If she's not interested in getting to know you, then why push?'

'Because she might change her mind.'

She might change her mind if I try hard enough... I wonder if the man who sent me and my friend unsolicited pizza and beer would have said the same thing. There's no way for me to reach out to him. After all these years, I don't even remember what he looked like. I never asked his name. But something tells me this is what he had in mind — that by being persistent, he could change our minds.

In and of itself, the idea that hard work and persistence pay off sounds noble. At work and in education, this may even work most of the time, if not all the time. But to apply the same principles to relationships seems a bit of a stretch. That being said, this approach to relationships is reinforced by our culture. In movies, it's almost a norm to see the hero in pursuit of a love interest with tactics not very different from the pizza and beers sent our way. Many young people get their idea of romance and relationships from movies. In reel life, with perseverance, the hero can woo the heroine. In real life, some men tend to emulate this method.

'I used to be a big SRK fan. I thought that there's only one love. Everyone has only one love, and you do everything you can to keep the love of your life happy. But I realized later there's no such thing. There are individual needs also. Everyone has their own life also,' Tushar confesses with a tinge of disappointment and amusement in his voice.

When parents pander to the whims of their children, they plant the seeds for this. Pandering is seen as an act of love.

'I don't see what's wrong with wanting my girlfriend to take an interest in the things I like,' Rachit wonders.

This is an ongoing fight between him and his girlfriend. He wants her to spend her weekends indoors, watching movies and playing video games. He also wants her to accompany him to all the parties his friends throw, which were quite frequent before the pandemic hit. She is not always up for it. She's neither a staying-in type of a girl nor a party girl. She likes being outdoors on weekends and in bed early regardless of whether it's weekend or weeknight. 'I want to experience these things with her. I want her to be a part of the things I enjoy doing.' Sounds lovely, until the things Rachit enjoys take his girlfriend away from the things *she* enjoys.

This idea that to be in love means to have identical lifestyles and interests is also quite common, Chandra tells me. 'Many men still think love means to be the same. But one has to understand that people have different experiences, opinions and preferences, and relationships are about finding the middle ground.'

The middle ground seems elusive though. From playgrounds, public transportation to universities and finally, marriage, none of these places is a 'middle ground' owned with equal authority by men and women. Nowhere is this disparity in our social structure as clear as it is in the institution of marriage. The premise of a marriage in our country is that the man and his family 'gain' a new member while the woman's family loses one. Wedding rituals like *kanyadaan* further solidify this by 'giving away' the bride. The woman becomes a commodity that the man 'gets'. No matter what we say, rituals aren't inconsequential. They build an ethos which leaves an imprint on our minds. That aside, the very practicalities of marriage reinforce this idea that a woman is something a man acquires. Chandra points this out when I ask him about the challenges of a new husband. He has to scramble to find patterns among newly married men. 'Men have to find the middle ground between the wife and the mother. They struggle to keep both women happy.' But for women, he says, 'there's a 360-degree change. Your address changes. The people you live with change. Even the food you eat is now what the husband's family eats. In many cases, women also change their last name. So a lot changes for the woman, not so much for the man.' (Obviously, these issues aren't there among couples who live on their own, but even today, in India, those are a minority). The woman, then, is expected to adjust around the man and his family, to do the 'fitting in' while men bask in having acquired a wife. Men aren't oblivious to this. Not at all. Men see this uneven keel, but most accept this as a fact of life rather than a structure that can maybe, one day, be broken down and rebuilt into a more egalitarian one.

I connect with Pradyum over a phone call a day before the 2021 lockdown begins. Pradyum is a chartered accountant from north-west Delhi. He lives with his mother, wife and two children. When I asked him if he was prepared for the lockdown, he said, '*Haan*, I'm prepared. I mean I don't have much to do. I just had to buy cigarettes and booze for myself. Groceries and stuff for the house, my wife and mother will take care of.'

In many Indian households, it's a given that the woman or women take care of the house. The men, at best, offer help when asked. When men feel entitled to women's care at home, it's bound to trickle into relationships as well.

Nikhil, a twenty-four-year-old man from an upper-middle class family in New Delhi, tells me young men should date because, 'The thing is, that's how you prove you're a man. I've known so many guys growing up who've been bullied for not being popular with girls. By the time you're fifteen–sixteen, if you don't have a girlfriend, you're considered a loser. It's like you're lagging behind.'

'So having a girlfriend is a competition?'

He nods. 'And an achievement.'

An achievement one is entitled to if they work hard enough. Michael Kimmel, in his book, *Guyland*, explains that men are in competition with other men.[4] Their actions are driven by wanting to outdo each other. The motto is to be better than the next man, whether it means having a higher pay cheque, a bigger car, more international trips or a bigger house. Sometimes it means having more sex with more women. Like Nikhil mentioned above, having a girlfriend is a competition and 'an achievement', just like your rank in college.

Men's lives seem to be built around acquiring — acquiring education that will qualify them for high-paying jobs, acquiring wealth that will qualify them for trophy wives, acquiring wives that will qualify them for respect.

SUCCESSFUL, POWERFUL AND ENTITLED

Circa 2013, I had opened a yoga studio and was taking on private clients other than the group classes I taught.

---

[4] Michael Kimmel, *Guyland* (Harper Perennial, HarperCollins, United States, 2008), p. 47.

The CEO of an advertising firm reached out to me and asked for personal classes at his house. My rule for one-on-one classes was that they would be held at my studio. But he cited a long commute and hectic work hours as reasons for not being able to come to my studio. They were legitimate reasons, so I considered his proposition, but finally, decided against it. The commute would have been long for me too, and the pay off wasn't worth it. A male friend cautioned me as I told him about my decision in a casual conversation. 'Be careful, though. Men like him are not used to taking no for an answer,' he said. I didn't know what to make of it then, and I don't know what to make of it now. He did take my refusal gracefully. But my friend's disclaimer may have had some basis in truth.

According to psychologists Jonathan Kunstman and Jon K. Maner, successful men overestimate their sexual attractiveness and the interest of others. Men with success, in its traditional sense of the word, assume that women are sexually interested in them even when they have no legitimate reason to believe so or facts to back the claim.[5] Psychologist Dacher Keltner writes in an essay titled, 'Sex, Power and the Systems That Enable Men Like Harvey Weinstein', 'Powerful men also sexualise their work, looking for opportunities for sexual trysts and affairs, and along the way, leer inappropriately, stand too close, and touch for too long on a daily basis, thus crossing the lines of decorum — and worse.'[6]

---

[5] Kunstman, J.W., Maner, J.K., 'Sexual overperception: power, mating motives, and biases in social judgment', *Journal of Personal and Social Psychology*, 2011

[6] Keltner, Dacher, 'Sex, Power, and the Systems That Enable Men Like Harvey Weinstein', *Harvard Business Review*, 3 October, 2017

Less than a decade later, workplace harassment at the hands of men in power has become cocktail party conversation, and the inspiration behind this book. #MeToo was set in action to put a stop to the abuse of this seat of power men hold in workplaces, and in the world at large. But the road hasn't been an easy one. Since the #MeToo movement came to India in October 2018, with Tanushree Dutta's allegations of sexual harassment against the Bollywood actor Nana Patekar, many men across industries were outed for having harassed female employees. We can't say if the movement has had a unified impact in any direction. Many different things have happened since: Some women were driven out of their jobs and forced to give up their career path because of continued harassment and lack of appropriate support systems. Some men have been held accountable and fired from their workplaces. Some have been ferociously fighting cases in court. Men are fighting back with cases of defamation. When journalist Priya Ramani was acquitted of defamation, as accused by M.J. Akbar, it was a victorious moment for #MeToo. Cut to 2021: Tarun Tejpal, former editor-in-chief of the popular publication *Tehelka*, was acquitted of a rape case filed against him in 2013. And we were once again questioning if women had any safe spaces to address their grievances.

Men are as torn about their thoughts on the matter as the movement has been. Some men feel apologetic on behalf of their clan. 'It's shocking to me that so many women have been facing this in silence. I feel really sorry for them and embarrassed to be a man when I hear such stories,' Viraj tells me. Viraj is a thirty-three-year-old independent artist who has his own set of professional frustrations. Having shuttled between Europe and India for five years now, he has been dealt harsh deals of racism as a Keralite during his travels.

But for some men, firing men from high paying jobs because of accusations of sexual harassment seems unfair. 'You can't ruin a man's career for this. He has spent years building his professional life and credibility and something like this should not take that away from him,' Tanuj, who is a marketing consultant at a multinational firm, tells me.

Entitled, then, to a successful career too.

SACRIFICE LEADS TO RESENTMENT LEADS TO ENTITLEMENT

Women's financial freedom has been the driving force behind many changes in gender roles in the last couple of decades. Being financially independent has meant that women can walk out of bad marriages even when they don't have family support, fight the pressure to get married by being able to afford to look after themselves, and finally, demand equal treatment in relationships. But these dual working relationships are a relatively new phenomenon, and many couples are the first in their family lineage where the woman too is out working. For many women, this means they now have two jobs — one at the office and one at home.

Nitin grew up watching his mother prepare meals for his father, have dinner ready when he would come home from work and not expect him to partake in household chores. His parents have been happily married for forty-three years. Nitin, thirty-three, is the youngest of three siblings. Newly married and living away from his parents for the second time in his life, he has had to make many 'unexpected adjustments'.

'If I have been out working for ten to twelve hours and I come home tired, is it unjustified for me to expect my partner to serve me food?' Nitin wonders aloud. Nitin is an earnest and hard-working man who takes pride in being a husband. Married for two and a half years, he has had to do a lot of unlearning and re-learning. 'It was difficult for my wife in the beginning. We used to fight a lot. We had a cook, but she would come in the mornings only. I like to come home and watch TV, just relax, you know? So, she was the one taking care of dinner. It led to a lot of fights. I would ignore her bickering.'

The lockdown forced Nitin to come face-to-face with the responsibilities of running a house. 'Now our cook is not coming at all. So we have to do everything. I don't like it. There's no need for us to live like this. I'm trying to convince my wife we should move in with my parents but she's not ready. So we are still fighting, but now I also help her with chores.'

I feel compelled to point out that in saying he 'helps around the house', Nitin still holds on to the idea that running the house is the wife's domain, and that he is entitled to living in a fully functioning home without putting in much effort.

According to Chandra, this tug of war between the new and the old ways of living and loving is the cause of many problems in our society.

For Nitin, and many others like him, who have subconsciously imbibed the gender stereotypes they grew up witnessing, the tug of war seems to be between being the provider versus being a partner for his wife. For our parents' generation, where the patriarch of the family being the sole provider was the norm, many men felt that since they were out working hard to make sure the family was well taken care of, their needs at home should be taken care of by the family. For many families and couples, like Nitin's parents, this arrangement worked. But children don't always understand such subtleties. They watch. They observe. They imbibe. They mimic. The byproduct of this is that many young boys have grown up mistakenly believing that they are entitled to a woman's care and attention just like their fathers were.

But what happens in double income relationships where the woman doesn't need to be provided for by the man? In many of these relationships, men still feel entitled to a woman's care. Monetary success seems to have been replaced by good behaviour, but the expectations, for some men, remain the same — that if they are nice to a woman, she should pander to his needs.

Pop culture definition of the 'nice guy syndrome' is this: A man who performs 'nice' deeds for women in expectation of a relationship or sex in return.[1] In other words, the 'nice guy syndrome' refers to men who feel entitled to a woman's attention or care because they do nice things for them without asking. These men, allegedly, get resentful when they are 'friend-zoned' by the women they like.

---

[1] Hosie, Rachel, 'The Sinister Logic Behind 'Nice Guy Syndrome', Explained by Psychologists', *The Independent*, 16 December 2016

In India, opposite sex friendships are still new and rare, and largely limited to metropolitan cities and some matrilineal groups. In some co-ed groups that are formed in school or college, there is a layer of segregation between boys and girls. They attend parties together, possibly take trips together, but when it comes to connecting at a deeper level, they sequester in same-sex sub-groups. Many don't believe in opposite sex friendships.

'There will always be some sexual tension between a guy and a girl. If not from both sides, then at least from one side. I don't think men and women can be friends like in the true sense,' twenty-seven-year-old Arjun, whom you'll meet again later, tells me in our elevator ride to the seventh floor where we share office space. Arjun is my former colleague. A pleasant guy with a good sense of humour, floppy hair and thick-rimmed glasses. Arjun and I would sometimes carpool to the office, and I thought we were friends. Like me, there were many other women Arjun used to hang out with and it seemed to me, was good friends with. Over the course of the next few months, I would find out that Arjun had slept with most of these women. They were friends... with benefits.

Arjun would sometimes flirt with me, and I would laugh it off as harmless banter. I liked his company but wasn't interested in any sort of benefits. Eventually, Arjun asked me out. We went on one date. I quickly realized there was no spark there, no potential and refused a second date. He distanced himself from me, and from carpool buddies, we became colleagues who didn't acknowledge each other's presence.

In hindsight, I realized we were never friends. He was planting the seeds for more, and when there was no seedling for him to reap, he abandoned the pot. Moved on to the next one, but not without resentment.

Neetu Sarin is a psychoanalyst based in Delhi. Just a few years my senior, she taught a semester as an ad hoc teacher when I was a student in Jesus and Mary College, Delhi University. Later, after I graduated, we became friends. Her first question about any guy I ever dated or was interested in would be: 'Does he have female friends?' She explained to me, 'How he is around women he isn't romantically or sexually involved with, will tell you how he really feels about women. Does he see women as friends or just romantic or sexual partners?'

Very few men in India see women as friends, and because of this, most men in India have what is called the 'nice guy syndrome'. Again, the roots of it are strengthened in childhood experiences when schools segregate boys and girls and parents tell young boys they can't play with girls or vice versa. When we pitch young children against each other because of sex and gender it carries on well into their adulthood.

Originally from a small town in Andhra Pradesh, Karthik has lived in four different cities, including Manipal where he was a student. 'We were ten years ahead of Delhi,' he tells me, speaking about his time at the university. 'When I moved to Delhi from Manipal in 2009, my approach with girls was different because in Manipal, we were very open. It was a melting pot. In Manipal, I had so many female friends. We would go for *pani puri* together, we'd get a beer.' He then points out that many people feel that you can do these things only with a girlfriend, not a friend. 'It's not that I didn't want a girlfriend. But it's okay. If it doesn't happen, it doesn't. I didn't feel like I was missing out on anything big.'

Normalizing opposite sex friendships then not only makes men feel less entitled to a woman's romantic or sexual involvement, it also humanizes women and men. Aren't we all ultimately people who just want *pani puri* and chilled beer?

PART TWO

Sexuality

Consent 101

'Nobody is born knowing how to say no. It's something we learn.'

— Lokesh, twenty-three

I remember a call I received from my best friend in the middle of a workday.

'I need a lawyer,' she had said as a manner of greeting. She then went on to narrate an unfortunate event that had happened to a friend of hers the night before. The friend — let's call her Z — had gone on a date with a young man she met on Tinder. As Tinder dates go, the two, after a couple of drinks, decided to go home together and started fooling around. However, Z did not want to consummate the liaison, and asked the man to stop. He didn't stop. 'He raped her, man,' my friend almost screamed into the phone. At the time, I told her I didn't think pursuing this legally was a wise decision. To me, it just didn't seem worth the scrutiny my friend's friend would be put through. Not to mention the painfully slow processes of the Indian judiciary.

While researching for this book, I reached out to lawyer and content creator, Tanya Appachu. As she informed me, 'There are no specific provisions in the Indian Penal Code [IPC] regarding date rape. There is no clarity provided by the courts on date rape. There have been cases where the courts have decided that the victim's "no" was not strong enough or it was very feeble and let go of the accused.[2] And there have been cases where the courts have held that consent should be expressed and can be withdrawn anytime.'

I ask her more about withdrawal of consent and how that may be dealt with in the legal system. Tanya tells me, 'In India, the courts have discussed implied and express consent in many cases. In the past it has been argued that usually a woman gives implied consent when she is in a romantic relationship or is a person of unchaste or immoral character, she hasn't screamed when she was raped, etc. So irrespective of arguments regarding implied and express consent, the Supreme Court [SC] has upheld implied consent is no consent, consent should be given expressly and out of free will. An explanation to Section 375 of the IPC states that consent in Indian law is revocable. That means consent has to be given for a specific sexual act engaged in and thus maybe subsequently withdrawn for something else. So consent once given can also be revoked, consent should be for a specific act and it should be given out of free will.'

But this is often not how things play out behind closed doors. And bringing violation of one's boundaries to the bedlam of a courtroom is not an easy or viable option for many. In fact, in many cases, dealing with the idea that one's boundaries may have been disregarded and

[2] Mahmood Farooqui, Criminal Law Appeal 944/2016 (Delhi High Court, 2017)

crossed is a long and arduous inner journey of confusion, shame and guilt. Especially in a romantic situation, the difference between implicit and express consent is not always easy to discern.

THE AZIZ ANSARI PHENOMENON

In a 2018 article that took the Internet by storm, writers at Babe.net published the story of 'Grace', a young, spirited woman — twenty-two at the time of this incident — who had an 'obnoxious' date with the funny, feminist Aziz Ansari. Grace met Ansari at an event where the two struck a conversation and exchanged numbers. They texted for a few weeks before Ansari invited her to dinner.

Speaking of the dinner, Grace shares that she had white wine even though she preferred red because Ansari ordered on her behalf. He rushed through clearing the cheque and hurriedly took her back to his apartment as soon as they were done with the perfunctory dinner. Once behind closed doors, any respect for boundaries seemed to elude this feminist comedian and writer. Grace described to the writer of the story, in detail, how Ansari overlooked Grace's body language and other non-verbal signs that she wasn't interested in a sexual encounter at the time. Even after she said, 'I don't want to feel forced,' Ansari allegedly didn't stop. When she could no longer take the 'obnoxious' behaviour, she left.

The next day, Grace texted Ansari that she had felt violated. Ansari later issued a public apology in which he stated that he misunderstood the events of that night and was surprised to hear that Grace had felt 'forced'.

Sexual coercion in the context of a date is a confusing and layered grey area. The reason why Grace's account hit home for many people is because it is all too common. Even though we now have intellectual conversations about consent — enthusiastic yes and non-verbal no's — there's still a lot left unanswered.

For example, do men pick up on the non-verbal signs? Do men think agreeing to go on a date is implicit consent for sex? Do they think they can change a woman's mind? Could it be that a woman's sexual coercion is a man's excellent persuasion skills?

'You can always tell if a girl is not interested in you by her body language,' twenty-five-year-old Peeyush Pandey tells me when I ask him about non-verbal signs of consent. He is a magician and practices martial arts. I ask him if his professional training makes him more attuned to people's body language and facial expression. 'Yes, yes, I think that's a factor. Even when I perform magic, it's all about gauging people's feelings through their facial expression. So yes, I think that makes a difference.'

Several men pointed out that their female partners are sometimes 'shy' in bed or don't like certain acts. 'Sometimes, I'll try to convince her to try out something new in bed, and I know that if I push for it, she will agree,' Tushar tells me, speaking of his wife. 'But I don't want to do that. I don't want to force her.'

Some men, though, feel resentful when their partners are unwilling to try out something new in bed or turn down their overtures. 'If I can't do it with my girlfriend, then who? Sometimes I know she's not into it and she does it only for me. But it's okay. I mean, I think we all do this for each other in relationships. Sometimes we do things we don't want to.'

Chandra tells me some men who come for couples therapy with their partner also complain that they can't be expected to be 'ready' when their partner wants to have sex. 'It happens sometimes. Women expect their partner to respect their boundaries, but when they want sex, they expect that men should be ready.' This is a byproduct of the myth that men are always on for sex.

Consent, then, is a two-way street. But the steering wheel has been handed over to men. Men are expected to woo women, and women to say yes or no. Female desire and agency is seldom talked about, whether in pop culture or locker room conversations. In recent years, thanks to OTT content competing with massy and mainstream cinema, we are seeing some progressive and realistic portrayals of women and what they want. Even now, the mainstream is dominated by toxic representations of the 'hero' — Kabir from *Kabir Singh* normalizing violence in the name of love; Bunny from *Yeh Jawaani Hai Deewani* claiming his right over Naina even though he's not ready to give her what she wants; Chulbul Pandey from *Dabangg* telling Rajjo not to grieve her father's passing because she is starting her new life with him.

Even in pop culture, men making decisions for women is the norm. The message men hear from movies like this, from family, friends and our very social fabric is that they don't need to ask. If a woman says no to something, they are well within their right to persuade her to change her mind.

When I was in my teens, boys following girls home on their bikes, making blank calls on their landlines and trying to find out information about the girls they found attractive through mutual friends was commonplace. Now, some of these behaviours are recognized as stalking.

Stalking is a punishable offence according to Section 35 D of the IPC. It is defined as any man following a woman and contacting a woman to foster a personal interaction despite repeated clear disinterest. It also includes electronic stalking, that is, monitoring a woman's use of any form of electronic communication like messages, emails, social media, etc. The punishment for stalking under IPC is up to three years imprisonment plus fine; and for a second or subsequent crime up to five years plus a fine. Under Section 67 of the IT Act, any person publishing or sending salacious material on electronic media amounts to obscenity. The punishment for this is up to five years imprisonment and a fine of Rs 1 lakh. Subsequent offence — ten years imprisonment plus 2 lakhs.

The National Crime Record Bureau (NCRB) published 'Crime Record' in the year 2020 with data collated up to 2018. As per the data there were 9,428 cases of stalking reported in the year 2018. That is, one case every 55 minutes on an average.

But stalking was recognized as a crime in the IPC only in the year 2013. So to a man who grew up in a diaspora wherein laws against harassment weren't yet established, where do the boundaries fall? Is he to go by the age-old trope of using his charms till the woman gives in or the modern rules of love where only yes means yes?

If only things were that black and white. Consent, or lack thereof, is not always just one word. It is sometimes in not knowing how to turn someone down, sometimes in ambivalence, and as Grace put it, sometimes, it sounds reluctant, like, 'I don't want to feel forced.'

Women sometimes succumb to sexual activity not because they are aroused or interested but because they are pressurized in subtle but unrelenting ways. Author Lois Pineau writes, '[Thus] while in principle, a firm unambiguous stand, or a healthy show of temper ought to be sufficient, if established, to show non-consent, in practice the forceful overriding of such a stance is apt to be taken as an indication that the resistance was not seriously intended, and that the seduction had succeeded.'[3]

In simple terms, merely saying 'no', regardless of what point of the interaction it comes at, should be enough. But is that how sexual encounters really play out? Not always. Some men persevere and take it upon themselves to break down the resistance. It becomes a challenge nobody gave them. The woman gives in, not because she has changed her mind thanks to his wheedling or persistence but because she fears the consequences of fighting back. Pineau explains, 'She does not adopt a strident angry stance, partly because she thinks he is acting normally and does not deserve it, partly because she feels she is partly to blame, and partly because there is always the danger that her anger will make him angry, possibly violent.'[4]

[3] L. Pineau, 'Date Rape: A Feminist Analysis', *Law and Philosophy*, 1998

[4] Ibid

Yes, this fear is legitimate. Think of all the cases of acid attack by rejected Romeos, and all the instances where boyfriends, either in fury or in passive aggressiveness or in a bid to act out the inner alpha male, fight back when their amour says that she does not want to continue the relationship. The chilling statement made by Mukesh Singh, one of the men convicted for the gruesome 2012 Delhi gang rape case, might shed light on the fear women live with. Here's what he said: 'When being raped, she shouldn't fight back. She should just be silent and allow the rape. Then they'd have dropped her off after doing her, and only hit the boy.'[5]

This is, by no means, only one man's viewpoint. In her book, *What We Talk About When We Talk About Rape*, Sohaila Abdulali narrates the harrowing incident of when she, much like Nirbhaya, was gangraped by four men while she was out with a male friend.[6] They too threatened to kill her if she didn't take what she had coming silently. This culture of silencing women using threats of violence is rampant, and it subsequently instils a deep fear in women which they have to carry around at all times. To be on high alert at all times.

This fear is instilled early on when young, hormonal schoolboys spread defamatory rumours about girls who refuse to go on a date with them. Or when possessive boyfriends threaten their girlfriends that they will release private conversations or details if they refuse to

[5] Udwin, L., A. Anand, A., A. In Singh, A., Krsna, *India's Daughter: The Story of Jyoti Singh*, Assassin Films, BBC Storyville (Firm), Danmarks radio, Women Make Movies (Firm), 2015

[6] Sohaila Abdulali, *What We Talk About When We Talk About Rape* (Penguin Random House India, New Delhi), 2018

comply with whatever their wishes may be. Or when manipulative bosses or husbands use their superior status to blackmail women they deem inferior and less powerful thanks to the misogyny imbibed in them by a sexist upbringing. *Quid pro quo.* The fear is not always that if a woman stands up against unsolicited advances she will be killed. It is that sometimes her dignity will be compromised, her character assassinated.

In May 2020, a Twitter user shared screenshots of a chat from 'Bois Locker Room', an Instagram group comprising teenage boys. It led to a heated controversy and nationwide discussion on how deep-rooted misogyny and rape culture is in India. The boys, who were mostly from affluent Delhi families and attended 'elite' schools, shared images of women — young teenage girls — made lewd, objectifying comments about them, going to the extent of discussing 'gang rape'. The leaked chat was horrifying, bringing to the surface the callousness with which men sometimes regard women. To think that even in 2020, educated boys with all the bells and whistles in place, would speak of women like they are meat makes one feel defeated.

Frustrated by the incident, I shared a news report on my Instagram stories. A thirty-something graduate of an elite South Delhi school responded to my story, defending Bois Locker Room. According to him, young boys trash talking women is a 'social learning', and shouldn't be curbed. That, while sharing morphed images was questionable, there was nothing wrong with the boys saying lewd things. 'By definition, locker room talk is dirty,' he goes on to say. After a heated debate, he asks me, 'How is a young teenage boy supposed to express his sexual desire, explore fantasies, if he can't even say these things privately to his friends?'

Speaking to *The Hindu*, Roma Kumar, a counselling psychologist at Ganga Ram Hospital, New Delhi, echoes the sentiment: 'As long as they are talking about sexual stuff, it should be fine because everybody talks about these things. We talk in a different manner, children are learning differently. But there should be some rules. We can't stop them, and we shouldn't stop them because it's a sexual energy that you are born with. But somebody has to be able to talk to these children in that manner, connect with them and also engage in conversations related to sexuality.'[1]

While expression of a systemically curbed, burgeoning sexuality is a part of the issue, as a woman, I can't un-see the threat such 'exploration' and 'social learning' poses to women. Banter may or may not lead to action, but it certainly creates a microcosm where women are degraded, disrespected and spoken of as objects to be consumed.

This is not to say that women are always victims and men are always the perpetrators of sexual violence. It is equally incorrect to assume or believe that consent is an issue that concerns only women; that men explore and act upon sexual desire while women are merely accomplices in an act.

In 2007, the Ministry of Women and Child Welfare, with support from United Nations Children's Fund,

---

[1] Ravi, Sidharth, 'Bois Locker Room, A Reflection Of An Existing Mindset', *The Hindu*, 21 May, 2020

conducted a study in which nearly 53 per cent of young children who reported abuse were boys. Between the years 2015 and 2019, the total number of child sexual abuse cases filed with Protection of Children from Sexual Offences (POSCO) in Kerala was 13,184. Out of these, 2,213 cases were of sexual abuse of young boys. The total number of male child victims was 2,250. This amounts to about 17 per cent of total child sexual abuse cases reported.[2,3]

When Lokesh started talking about his sexual abuse on public forums, something unexpected happened. Men in large numbers started writing to him about their own experiences with sexual trauma. They wrote to him in confidence, believing he would understand. Lokesh is young — only twenty-three — and his youthfulness is evident in his friendly and approachable online presence. The intention behind these confessions he regularly receives in his inbox is not to get guidance or healing but to simply share, find validation and a companion in their suffering. By telling Lokesh their stories, these men, in their private rooms, are softly whispering, 'Hey, #MeToo.'

I ask Lokesh why he thinks men feel reluctant talking about abuse in public. One reason he tells me is that they don't want to bring shame to their families. 'There's a fear of being judged. That plays a huge role. Men fear being judged and shamed for their sexuality.'

---

[2] Subramaniyan, Vyjayanthi Kanugodu Srinivasa et al. 'Silence of male child sexual abuse in India: Qualitative analysis of barriers for seeking psychiatric help in a multidisciplinary unit in a general hospital', *Indian Journal of Psychiatry*, 2017

[3] TNN, 'Boys are Victims in 17% Child Sexual Abuse Cases in Kerala', *Times Of India*, 9 November 2020

50 SHADES OF CONSENT

Consent matters. Everyone has the right to decide what they want to do, or have done, with their body. Any violation of boundaries is abuse and can have irreversible adverse affects on one's mental health. Unintentional violation of one's sexual boundaries due to a lack of awareness or miscommunication causes stress, anxiety and depression in women and men as often as deliberate sexual abuse does. In fact, sometimes more severely, precisely because it does not fit the description of sexual assault in absence of consent. It's confusing and makes one doubt themselves. It goes beyond physical assault and enters the realm of emotional and psychological manipulation. Despite the grave psychological consequences of abuse, consent isn't something we are taught about or talk about enough. 'Nobody's born knowing how to say no,' Lokesh points out. 'This is something we learn.' And this holds true for all genders, not just for women.

This is why it falls upon *everyone* to break this communication barrier and start talking about their sexual needs and boundaries. To help each other say no. We're still a long way from this. Many couples who end up in Chandra's clinic are unable to communicate their boundaries to their partner. 'If you don't exert your boundaries, you also normalize the idea that it's okay for you to not enjoy sex,' he tells me. I point out to him that sometimes women say no, and their male partners get angry. 'Yes, that happens,' he says. 'I would say, if he gets angry, let him. Let it be.'

Part of this anger comes from the fact that men see taking a no as a sign of weakness or as unmanly. The other part comes from confusion around what's appropriate and what's not or assumptions about consent. 'If a girl comes over to my house after a date,' Ayaaz tells me, 'I would assume she's up for sex. Isn't "you want to go home?" code for "you want to have sex?",' he wonders.

But it's exactly this code language that we need to break. Below is a non-exhaustive list of things that are *not* a code for sex:

1. Going home with someone
2. Flirting
3. Having dinner or drinks
4. Talking about sex or sexuality
5. Having sex with other people
6. Being attracted to you
7. Making out with you. One can change their mind at any point.
8. Having had sex with you before
9. Being in a relationship with you
10. Consenting to one type of sexual act doesn't mean consenting to all types of sexual acts

Here's the golden rule of consent: Consent is continuous and enthusiastic and can be retracted at any time.

But are things as clear in practice? Not always. Women are sometimes too shy to say no. And some men may feel saying no means they aren't masculine enough. Sometimes a man may be too awkward to ask upfront. Or too pushy, presumptuous, entitled or simply ignorant about body language and other non-verbal and verbal cues. It may also be that one or both of the parties play gendered roles in sexual dialogue — the coy, inhibited woman waits for a man to take her, while the man puts on a proud show of his virility. We live in a society that heavily favours one gender (no brownie points for guessing which one), all the while dictating (or at least trying to) the etiquette of the other. One of the consequences of allowing men to take the lead in sexual matters is that women sometimes suppress their desire in order to feed the male-dominated ideal of the 'pure' woman. In a culture where virginity tests as eligibility criteria for prospective brides are not frowned upon, it shouldn't be surprising that women either deny that they should have any sexual desire outside the bounds of a marriage, or if they do, they underplay it lest they are judged for 'having loose morals'. For instance, Tushar's wife wanted to wait till they got married to have sex. They dated for years before they tied the knot, but sex happened only after their relationship was solemnized. They would make out whenever they visited each other, he tells me.

Other times, women succumb to the man's desires to protect themselves. This is often the case in situations like a date where there may be sexual ambivalence, as was the case with Aziz Ansari. At some level, in some way, with a man who may or may not be a self-proclaimed feminist, many women have felt coerced and trapped in an unwanted sexual encounter. Sometimes women view sex as a chore and want to get it over with.

While researching for an article on why women fake orgasms, I came across Akanksha. Akanksha is a mom of two chatty young girls — eight and six. As a response to my post online, she tells me she often fakes it with her partner 'to make him feel he did a good job. I have no energy for round two, his ego is pampered. All win.' I ask her if she thinks her partner would feel bad if she was honest with him. She tells me he tries to make her climax, but she has 'lost her libido'. I ask if we can speak on the phone.

It's day one of lockdown 2.0 and her daughters are arguing in the background. 'My MIL wants us to have a son,' she tells me. 'Every time I make out with my husband, I fear that her God will listen to her prayers for a grandson,' she laughs.

'So I was telling you... It's very difficult to say no to a man, ya. *Pyaar, vyaa*r...compassion, men don't have that. My husband you know...he doesn't talk to me if I tell him I'm not in the mood. I'll say let's do it tomorrow. Next day, he'll refuse. It becomes a competition for him. I'll refuse, then he'll say no. It's become a joke.'

'Mumma, Maira is not giving me my slinky!' Her daughter complains in the background.

'Maira! You give her what she wants!' she says to her daughter, and then to me, 'Sorry! If you're writing about these things, here's what you should write about — my father was in the ICU with COVID and my husband just wanted to have sex.' She lowers her voice. I assume she does this so her daughters can't hear. 'I told him I can't and this man takes it personally. But it's not about you. My father just got out of the hospital. Everyone in my family tested positive, and he still thinks it's about him!'

Her daughters get louder in the background. 'Mumma! Look at what Maira is doing.'

'Maira! Not now! Please give me two minutes!'

Akanksha has more to tell me. '*Kuchh ho jata inko* (something happens to men). Men can't take it when we say no. Something — I don't know what it is. For my husband, sex is like cricket. Or exercising. He just does it. So I also just do it. Even when I don't enjoy it.'

Sometimes, one genuinely doesn't know if they want to go forward with a sexual act. One may be confused. Simply put, in practicality, one doesn't always get to hear a firm 'no', or a clear 'yes'. So what does one do in such a situation? Ignore the mixed signals and carry on anyway?

There are two things that are happening here: one is confusing or inauthentic behaviour that emanates from social conditioning, and the other, sexual ambivalence that emanates from genuine not-knowing. Both men and women need to lift the veil of silence and break away from sexual conditioning, own the confusion when it arises and communicate.

Chandra says that it if we want to change how people approach sex and sexuality, it is crucial that we learn how to communicate. 'The most important thing when it comes to sexuality is communication. It is restricted because of the fear of being judged or compared. We need to get over this,' he advices. He insists that there is no black or white in relationships. It's all grey, and we have to be okay with grey areas. 'We must always strive to find the middle ground. And if we can't find the middle ground, we must learn to agree to disagree.'

For many couples, openly communicating about sex doesn't come easy. Our culture doesn't equip us to talk about sex. This is when it becomes imperative to get help if needed instead of accepting this as how things are.

WHEN ONE PERSON WANTS MORE, WHAT DO YOU DO?

Sexual boundaries in the context of a relationship are sometimes pushed because of different sexual appetite and preferences. No two people, no matter how sexually compatible, can always be on the same page about everything. One may like fifteen minutes of foreplay, whereas the other may be okay with just about a minute or two. One may like to receive oral sex more than give or vice-versa. One may prefer one position over another.

Sexual appetite is not defined by one's genitals, and men too have preferences, moods and fluctuations in their desire for sex. Like Pradyum, a doting husband and father, told me, 'Men have headaches too!'

Between two people who have been together for a considerable amount of time, there may arise times when one partner succumbs to the needs of the other, but at no point should this come at the cost of one's emotional well-being and respect for each other. Chandra points out that you can judge the quality of your relationship by how well you can communicate your mood to your partner. 'If you're not in the mood, you should be able to tell your partner.'

The only way to keep your relationship strong is to keep the communication strong. What is okay and what is not in your relationship is only for you and your partner to decide. As a rule of thumb, if there is something you want to do in bed and your partner is not keen on it, discuss the possibility once or twice and then drop the issue. If there is something new you are trying, come up with a safe word and honour it when it is used. Be cognizant of each other's mental states even in bed. Sex in a relationship is often more than just the act, but rather, a culmination of the entirety of your interactions. When you make love to someone you are romantically involved in, it is almost impossible to ignore the quality of your relationship with them. The arguments, disappointments and resentments don't suddenly disappear when a couple has sex. Nor do love and care. Connecting purely at a physical level may be ambitious when you are also connected at an emotional level.

CONSENT MATTERS IN ALL AREAS OF LIFE, NOT JUST SEX

Madhumita Pandey, a scholar who has interviewed 100 convicted rapists in Tihar Jail, Delhi, says, 'Men are learning to have false ideas about masculinity and women are also learning to be submissive. It is happening in the same household. Everyone's out to make it look like there's something inherently wrong with [rapists]. But they are a part of our own society. They are not aliens who've been brought in from another world.'

At the root of sexual violence is sexism — the idea that people have different mechanisms of behaviour and must be treated differently based on their sex. Rape is the extreme along the spectrum of biased and prejudiced beliefs and values that place less value on one gender (female). There may be many theories about why men rape — sexual frustration, power, psychological illness, lack of education and knowledge, but we can't divorce any of these theories from the gender politics involved in sexual crimes. Gender-based violence falls along the same spectrum as sexist jokes, the butt of which is the female, but it is just on the other end. The common thread between these behaviours is a dehumanization of the female.

Sexism, and its expressions, are multi-layered and complex. Often, it comes in gender-neutral language, decorated with gendered accents. It comes in the form of pink walls for young girls and blue for young boys. Barbie dolls and G.I. Joe's. Skirts and dresses and Bermuda shorts. Fairy tales that shamelessly teach that women need a Prince Charming and superheroes who are almost always men. That boys don't cry. It comes in the form of 'protective' mothers and fathers who don't allow their daughters to date, while the son has many girlfriends. Or in the idea that while a woman may be doing well for herself, she must marry a man who does better than her or not marry at all! And the over-glorification of motherhood that carefully cloaks the sacrifices a woman makes to raise a child and systematically alienates the man — the father. There is sexism everywhere if you stop and pay attention.

Much of it contributes to our abysmal lack of understanding of consent. Because, honestly, sexual consent is simply a reflection of how much you value one's autonomy in any area of life. If one truly — at a deeper emotional level, not just intellectually — believes a woman is her own person, with her own body, mind and soul, free to make her own choices, this *will* reflect in their sex life too.

'I have specialized in sexuality studies but even then I always say we don't need to understand sex separately,' Chandra tells me. 'How we treat our sexual needs is a reflection of how we approach our needs in other aspects of life. We remain the same person.'

Let's Talk about Sex, Baby!

'Sex is no fun if both of us are not having fun.'
— Vidur, twenty-seven

A 2017 STUDY PUBLISHED IN the *Archives of Sexual Behaviour* shows the gnawing gap between men and women in heterosexual relationships achieving climax.[4] The men interviewed in this study demonstrated that they are on the hot seat in matters of lust, given that they reported having an orgasm 95 per cent of the time. The women, on the other hand, lingered at an abysmal 65 per cent! Many fake it. A few men I spoke to, however, claimed that they can tell when a woman fakes an orgasm. But they just didn't care.

'If she's faking it, then I also fake it for her,' thirty-three-year-old Harsh tells me over WhatsApp. I can picture him smirking, laughing at his own clever joke. I ask him to explain what he means. 'If she doesn't care about her own pleasure, why should I?'

Harsh's comment is a disclaimer for women. Women must learn to take ownership of their sexual pleasure and

---

[4] Frederick, D.A., John, H.K.S., Garcia, J.R. et al., 'Differences in Orgasm Frequency Among Gay, Lesbian, Bisexual, and Heterosexual Men and Women in U.S.', *Archives of Sexual Behaviour*, 2017

learn to hold men accountable. But with sexuality cloaked in so many layers of shame, guilt, ignorance, this isn't always easy. Sometimes though it's not about the ease.

Mani has perfected her fake moans and contorted orgasm face. At only twenty-six, this charming Mumbai girl has decided that sometimes it's not worth fighting for pleasure when it comes to sex. She is a sales executive and has admirable persuasion skills when it comes to her clients. But with men, she resorts to faking it. 'I fake it a lot. I don't think it's always a bad thing. Sometimes you just know it won't happen. That could be because the sex just isn't that good or the guy is too into himself. So I fake it to get it over with.' She smiles like a mischievous kid who knows she's done something she shouldn't have. I suspect there's more Mani has to share. I don't need to probe though. She tells me of her own volition. 'So I have a trick. To get the guy to come quickly so we can all move on with our lives.' With that grin intact on her face, she tells me, 'Just do kegels when he's inside you. The contractions will give him a push and he'll be done in a few seconds.'

CAN PLEASURE EXIST WITHOUT INTIMACY?

The clitoris contains more than 8,000 nerve endings the purpose of which is solely pleasure.[5] Yet, pleasure is elusive to many women. The 'complex' female anatomy is used as a convenient excuse by some men. 'With guys it's simple,' Harsh explains. 'You just focus on the tool

[5] Thomasan, Kristine, '10 Things You Never Knew about the Clitoris', *Health*, 5 October 2015

and that's it. Nothing is hidden. But women's bodies are different.'

And that's just the point. Women's bodies *are* different. But the problem is not that the female body is complex, it is that some men don't care enough to learn about it. Like Mani pointed out, 'Pleasure is different from woman to woman. Our bodies are different. And many men have a bad attitude about learning about women's bodies. Like they don't like being taught because they feel being taught means they don't know how to pleasure a woman.'

For many men and women who are in their adulthood at the time of writing this book, sex education has come from pop culture and porn. This, combined with a lack of open conversation, has led many to believe that a woman can easily achieve an orgasm through vaginal stimulation alone, often leaving them unsatisfied. But to give credit where it's due, some men do try to be creative when stimulating the vagina. A few examples are — spiralling your way in and out, thrusting hard and rhythmically, manoeuvering the penis while inside so that it touches the walls. While these movements feel pleasurable, they don't always lead to an orgasm. The reason is that most women achieve orgasm through clitoral stimulation. Not many men know this.[6] And how would they? After all, most sex scenes in movies and pornography — where majority of our sex education comes from — show a woman reaching climax in all her panting, breathless glory, from the

[6] Koedt, Anne, '*The Myth Of The Vaginal Orgasm*', City University of New York Academic Commons, 1970

man having been inside. Of course, vaginal orgasms are not entirely mythical. They do happen. But not as commonly or smoothly as men and women have been led to believe by sweaty actors. To put things in perspective, a recent study conducted in America revealed that while nearly 37 per cent women achieve orgasm by clitoral stimulation, the number of vaginal orgasms was only 18 per cent.[7] In India, the extent of sexual dysfunction is difficult to measure or estimate because most Indian women still don't seek help for sexual problems.[8]

To be clear though, an orgasm is not all in the clitoris. Or all in the body. Studies show that women report higher sexual satisfaction with intercourse in a relationship compared to random hook ups.[9] The likelihood of reaching an orgasm is also higher when you are in a relationship. One of the reasons for this may be that in a relationship, we know each other's bodies and preferences better and so are able to pleasure each other more satisfactorily. But this comes with a disclaimer. It's not one's relationship status or commitment that enhances sexual pleasure. It's *connection.* A sense of emotional closeness that allows for authentic verbal and non-verbal communication. This is also true for some men. Like some women, some men also want

---

[7] Herbenick, Debby, Fu, Tsung-Cheih, Arter, Jennifer, Sanders, Stephanie A., & Dodge, Brian, 'Women's Experiences With Genital Touching, Sexual Pleasure and Orgasm', *Journal Of Sex & Marital Therapy*, 2018

[8] Nilanchali Singh, Pallavi Sharma, Neha Mishra, 'Female Sexual Dysfunction: Indian Perspective and Role of Indian Gynecologists', *Indian Journal Of Community Medicine*, 2020

[9] Armstrong, Elizabeth A., England, Paula, Fogarty, Alison C. K., 'Accounting for Women's Orgasm and Sexual Enjoyment in College Hookups and Relationships', *American Sociological Review*, 2012

to feel a connection and be in the right mental space for sex. Ishan finds casual sex boring. At thirty-three, he's divorced and living alone in the apartment he and his wife set up together. Since the formalization of his divorce in late 2017, he's been meeting and hooking up with a lot of women. 'Casual sex is fun but after a point, it's all the same. The real intimacy is when you can have a conversation before or after sex.' This doesn't mean he would stop hooking up casually. 'I'm single now, so why not? But I'm only fulfilling a physical need. There will be no need for all this if I meet someone I can be with. That's not happening right now, so why stop myself from getting laid?'

'There has to be some intellectual compatibility. It is very important for me to be able to have a conversation with the woman before I can have sex with her,' Aadil tells me. Aadil is a young lawyer. He doesn't have the time for a serious relationship, he tells me. But he doesn't want to spend his twenties as an ascetic either. He is a regular user of dating apps. As things go on dating apps, it isn't uncommon for people to have sex with a match before they have a date (if at all). 'Not that I don't hook up. But it's so much better when there's some connection.'

The act of sex is as diverse as sexuality. Everybody can have casual sex given the right circumstances. And everybody can stay monogamous. But the same actions can have very different meanings for different people — for women and men.

Recently, I reconnected with a long-lost pen friend. He reached out to me because he was going through heartbreak and wanted to talk to someone distant, but safe. Someone he felt connected to but who wasn't involved in his day-to-day life. 'I'm trying very hard to wrap my head around this,' he tells me over the phone. We are pen friends from the snail mail era, and this is the first time we've heard each others' voices. He has a baritone, and I can't help but wonder what he looks like. Is he tall? Dark? Handsome? Is his hair thick and long or does he sport a crew cut? He sounds like he has a crew cut and a chiseled jaw. Perhaps a goatee. I resist the temptation to Google him because I want to preserve this old-school friendship where only what was shared was known.

Not unlike how he wanted to preserve old-school romance in his relationship. But his erstwhile lover wanted to open up the relationship, to experiment, explore, sleep with other men. 'I get it. She's young. *We* are young. She wants to explore. I don't judge her at all. And I don't want to stop her from doing it. But I…I can't be with her while she explores.'

Another friend — a male in his early thirties — had a similar story, but he chose to go with it. Though he decided to stay exclusive, he was okay with his partner exploring her sexuality, which meant being sexually involved with other men. They eventually got married. His wife has decided to be monogamous for now.

Sonal is the younger of two sisters raised in a *baniya* family in Delhi. Her sister is fair and pretty, she tells me. 'But look at me,' she points to her dusky face. 'My mother would always say, "*Tu toh kitni kaali hai. Shaadi kaun karega tujhse?*" (You have such a dark complexion. Who will marry you?).' She got married young, to the 'first decent guy' who didn't mind her dark complexion.

After nine years and two children, she left her husband. It was a loveless marriage, as many arranged marriages are, and after having had two children, at the age of thirty-four, she fell in love with someone else. After a year-long affair that she initially kept under wraps, she decided to walk out on her husband to be with her lover, Vikas. Her lover was also married (unhappily) at the time they met.

Monogamy and loyalty, as I learnt, have little to do with one's sex or gender. The difference, however, lies in how we perceive male versus female desire. We believe men are driven by sexual desire and are naturally more inclined to have multiple sexual partners, while we believe that women are naturally inclined to monogamy. Women, then, tend to be more secretive of their dalliances, while men are less afraid of being public.

During the one year that Sonal was seeing Vikas, she would insist on meeting in private. Hotel rooms. Vacation homes. The most public place she was okay with being seen with Vikas was at his best friend's house. This was a sore point in their relationship as Vikas wanted more — he wanted to take his girlfriend out to clubs, dinners and movies. 'I wanted my wife to find out. That would've made it easier to get her to divorce me,' he told me when I asked if he wasn't worried about being seen with another woman. On the other hand, Sonal was worried that if her husband — or anybody else — found out about her affair, they would judge her character and make divorce proceedings needlessly difficult. She wanted the divorce first, and then come out about her relationship with Vikas.

In September 2019, my girlfriends and I went on a trip to Goa. We got acquainted with a group of three men. Two were married with kids. One was single. The married men showed me and my companion pictures of their wives and children on their phones. 'She is the love of my life! I can't live without her,' one told us. It was endearing. Later that evening, they had escorts arriving from Delhi. The single man had opted out of flying in a foreign woman for a paid 'girlfriend experience', so there were only two escorts — one for each of the two married men.

'*Apne laundon ke saath vacation pe aaye hain, toh kuchh mazaa toh karna chahiye na*! (We're on vacation with the boys. We must have some fun!),' they explained. The single friend stole a moment away with me later and told me, 'They feel cool and relevant when they do things like this. I think it's some strange sense of achievement.'

This idea that having a woman for company is an achievement — just like getting a promotion — comes up often.

RELEASE AND REJOICE

When Ashish Bisht's grandfather passed away, all he could think of was finding a private spot in his house flooded with relatives in mourning so he could masturbate. He was close to his grandfather growing up and was deeply pained by his passing. Yet even before the relatives dispersed back to their homes, all he wanted was sexual release. 'It was one of my lowest moments,' he tells me. 'I feel ashamed talking about it.

But at that time, I felt desperate. Like a drug, I had to do it. So I locked myself in the bathroom and jerked off.'

As the second wave of COVID-19 swept across our country, Varun's parents also contracted the deadly virus. In their late sixties, both had to be admitted to a private nursing home on day five of the illness. Varun would be on his toes all day, making visits to the nursing home, delivering food and ensuring his parents received adequate care. At night, once he'd had dinner and survived another day of keeping his parents alive, he would want to have sex with his wife. 'During that week, the sex was very mechanical. I know my wife didn't like that at all. And maybe it's…perverted of me to want sex when my parents are in the ICU. But it's a physical release. It helped me go to sleep at night.'

But the release that comes from sex isn't always an antidote to morbidity. Vidur is a sales executive with an American firm with its offices in Gurugram. He has a high-pressure job with ambitious sales targets and virtual meetings that are often in different time zones. He is currently casually dating a colleague in a similar role. 'She lives with her family, so after work, we come to my place and hang out.' Vidur's family is in Ludhiana, and he lives in a tall tower in Gurugram with two other people — a man in his early twenties, and a woman in her late twenties. All three moved to the corporate hub in pursuit of jobs. 'It's all casual. We are just hooking up with each other. Neither of us wants more.' The two have talked about this and have come to the agreement that if things ever start to get emotional, they will call it quits. 'But you know, if I don't get laid for a week, I can see it affecting my work. I can't concentrate.'

When Vidur seals an important deal at work, he likes to celebrate with his friend with benefits (FWB). Meaning they get dinner and drinks and end the night with sex. This is unusual for them. Usually, it's a hurried drink or two before they get down to business and each go their separate ways for mealtime. 'Those kind of days are special. I want to celebrate my win. I'm feeling successful and like a winner. Getting laid on those days makes me feel like more of a winner.' And what if his FWB has had a bad day? 'It's never happened. She's smart,' he sniggers. I insist he hypothesize. 'I'd be bummed. That would be really shitty. But I'd then see if one of my matches on Hinge or Bumble is free to meet. I don't know,' he shrugs. 'At least I'll get a date, if not sex.'

Many regrettable hook ups with exes seem to happen because of this impulse to use sex to release or rejoice. Akshay Bhasin is a techie based in Bengaluru. Three months after breaking up with his long-time sweetheart, he put in his papers at Google to start his own company with two other friends. It was a night of celebration and anxiety. After walking out of the coveted Google office, he met his partners at Hard Rock Cafe for drinks. 'Even after seven to eight beers, I was wide awake. I didn't want to go to an empty, depressing house. For some reason, I really missed Aditi that night. I texted her and she invited me to her house. It got awkward after that because she wanted to try one more time, and I didn't.'

My guess is that night marked his first step into an unfamiliar world. With so much about his future left to the imagination, he wanted something that felt familiar and certain. As certain as an ex's familiar touch.

MEN WANT TO FEEL DESIRED TOO

There is another pervasive myth about male sexuality — that men have a natural inclination to being in charge. During my conversations with men, broaching this topic often opened a can of worms. If to be a man is to desire, then what does it mean for a man to be desired?

It depends.

When a man is desired, it feeds his self-esteem and the idea of what he thinks he should be. 'I felt like a real man,' Akshat, who was popular with the ladies at his college, tells me. 'I had all these girls who wanted me, and I could take my pick. It was a power trip.' Akshat is now twenty-seven, single and looking for someone to fall in love with. 'It changes as you grow older. I think girls become more picky [*sic.*].' I ask him if he's become pickier with age. 'I have become less of a hopeless romantic. All girls are the same. As in, you can be with anybody. But I think most girls have attitude problems these days.'

I realized that the deflection to the supposed 'attitude problem' among women was Akshat's way of not talking about the sense of inadequacy now that it's become more difficult for him to date women. It seemed easier to assume women in their mid-twenties are fussy than acknowledge that the dating pool shrinks for everyone with age and maybe he could do something about it.

It's one thing to not be desirable in the dating pool, but a whole different ball game when one is, or feels, undesirable in a relationship. For thirty-three-year-old Parikshit, this led to habitual masturbation, which he 'didn't even enjoy'. Parikshit has a corporate job and lives in Gurugram with his wife. The first year of their marriage was 'great fun', he tells me. Then his wife began losing interest in sex. Parikshit opened up about this over e-mail. We had spoken on the phone a few times before he sent me his diary entry. It read:

'It happened again. I asked. She agreed. I moved. She froze. I feel I am using her when she becomes uninvolved like that. She is my wife. I love her, and I want her to enjoy it with me, to feel the same pleasure I feel when I enter her. I stopped. I went to the washroom, stood under the shower and masturbated. I don't know what happened — I began crying.'

Parikshit and his wife have been seeing a couple's counselor. 'I still find it difficult to talk about this,' he told me. 'But at least now I know what is happening. I used to get so angry at my wife for this. We would have horrible fights. She also has to work on herself. She feels too shy.'

A woman's honour is usually tied with curbing her sexuality; similarly a man's masculinity is about flaunting it. While a woman must protect her honour by keeping her legs closed, quite literally, a man must demonstrate his manhood by putting on a show of his sexuality. How can the one physical act that bridges the gap between men and women be so disparate in its meaning for the two sexes? This just goes out to show that patriarchy doesn't want its men and women to coexist in peace and harmony, but rather just survive in each other's company with an undercurrent of hostility.

Both men and women must strive to free themselves from such gendered perspectives, and find their own, individual sexual map. There's nothing honourable about virginity or prudence or masculine about the number of women one has slept with. Sexuality is as similar, and diverse, as men and women are. Both men and women have sexual urges. Both experience orgasms. Both feel frustrated when they are sexually starved. Both hurt when they feel unattractive. Both feel confident when they feel attractive. But each person has his or her own sexual boundaries and proclivities. The key is to honour both — the similarities and the differences between men and women and individuals regardless of their sex.

Sex is about pleasure, not power, compliance or domination. In our society, sex is viewed as a duty for women and an innate need for men. The man's job is to desire and conquer while the woman complies. Chandra tells me there is a dire need to see sex as more than just a physical act. 'It's not just for physical satisfaction,' he says. 'If it's about sexual release for you, there are many ways to get that satisfaction or release — you can masturbate, you can use toys. There is no harm in these things. In a relationship, or when you are with another person, sex is more than a physical act.'

THE GROWING BREED OF MEN WHO WANT TO PLEASURE THEIR WOMAN

'Sex is no fun if both of us are not having fun,' Vidur had told me. In his mid-twenties, the perky young man belongs to the future generation of husbands and fathers. Emblematic of upward mobility in modern India, he is a representation of what the future has in store for us. Working a well-paying job, setting up his own home away from his parental home and with the best technology on his fingertips, he is at once in tune with many different worlds. He points out, 'Everyone has the same information. We are all watching the same stuff online. There are so many conversations happening about consent, sex — it's all fine now. Men of my generation — or even women — don't see sex as bad or anything.'

He is right about two things, wrong about one. Let's look at what he got right.

One-third of the Indian population has access to the internet. Anything that's published online can potentially be viewed by anyone anywhere. Yes, there are many conversations going on about consent and sexuality — normalizing female agency, pleasure and mutuality in sex. The men who consume this kind of content are, indeed, imbibing it. They are learning that there's nothing wrong with sex or a woman who enjoys sex. They are also learning that caring about a female partner's pleasure is a desirable trait. They are also learning that a man who appreciates a woman's boundaries, fantasies and agency is desirable. These men see sex as what it is — fun and pleasurable — and they want sexual encounters to be fun and pleasurable for everyone involved.

'If only I'm having fun, and if it's only about me finishing, then I might as well jack off. Why put in so much effort?' Twenty-five-year-old Robin from Jaipur thinks if sex is not enjoyable for everyone, it's wasted.

But it's more than just a fun activity. Pleasuring one's partner also seems to boost some men's self-image, just like it does for some women. They feel they have succeeded. They've done a good job. Whether that's altruistic or comes from a sense of accomplishment is open to interpretation.

'I feel good when I make her feel good,' Vidur reminds me as our chat comes to an end. But there's something he got wrong. While most people have access to the internet, not everyone consumes content that attempts to normalize sex and sexuality.

Esther Perel, a Belgian psychologist and author who has given us remarkable insights on desire, infidelity and modern relationships, has also taught us that male sexuality is, indeed, greatly emotionally and relationally driven. Talking about performance anxiety, fear of rejection and insecurity, she states, 'They seep directly into his sexual self, his desires, and fantasies.' She further goes on to talk about how a man's sexual identity is tied with satisfying his partner. Turning her on is a turn-on for him primarily because her being involved makes him feel less predatory.[1]

The conversation with Robin steers towards this idea. He tells me, 'I feel like I've used her when she doesn't enjoy it.' There are times, he says, when he finishes before her. When this happens, he offers to satisfy her in other ways.

Men like Robin and Vidur are changing the sexual script from 'when the man finishes, the sex finishes'.

SEXUAL DYSFUNCTIONS

While speaking to men and women about sex and sexuality, I realized that women tend to share stories of discomfort, awkwardness, encroached boundaries

[1] Perel, Esther, 'Men, Women And Sexuality: More Similar Than Different', estherperel.com

and missed orgasms while men tend to share stories of conquest. Sometimes, this conquest is a solo pursuit, where the woman is the one to be won over; at other times, it's about pleasure, a joint effort between men and women.

Women are frequently troubled by what is called Female Sexual Dysfunction (FSD). FSD is a cluster of problems associated with female desire, arousal, orgasm and satisfaction. If one has FSD, they exhibit little of one or two or all of the above. And it is extremely common. Colloquially called 'frigidity', far too many women suffer from problems with either feeling desire or being aroused even with proper stimulation or reaching an orgasm or feeling satisfied post-coitus. In one study, 40.9 per cent of the women were diagnosed with FSD.[2] Another study pits the number at 46.2 per cent.[3] And another at 43 per cent.[4] Surely such a large number of women can't have a clinical issue that is purely biological, and if indeed this is the case, why is it that it's not making headlines and invoking a public cry for help?

This is because FSD is not purely a biological phenomenon. It is as much cultural as it is psychological. One of the biggest problems is that lack of sexual proclivity in women is considered normal in our society.

---

[2] McCool, Megan E., Zuelke, Andrea, Theurich, Melissa A., Knuettel, Helge, Ricci, Cristian, Apfelbacher, Christian, Prevalence Of Female Sexual Dysfunction Among Premenopausal Women: A Systematic Review And Meta-Analysis Of Observational Studies', *Sexual Medicine Reviews*, 2016

[3] Jaafarpour, Molouk, Khani, Ali, Khajavikhan, Javaher, Suhrabi, Zeinab, 'Female Sexual Dysfunction And Risk Factors', *Journal Of Clinical And Diagnostic Research*, 2013

[4] Allahdadi, Kyan J., Tostes, Rita C.A., Webb, R. Clintonn, 'Female Sexual Dysfunction: Therapeutic Options And Experimental Challenges', US National Library of Medicine, National Institutes Of Health, 2009

It is falsely assumed that women have lower libido than men. Yes, women go through many hormonal changes throughout the month and their libido fluctuates whereas a man's remains more or less constant. But it would be wrong to equate fluctuations with lesser desire. The same can be said for arousal — using lubrication is seen as a convenient alternative when women find it difficult to be aroused. Often, a woman's pleasure does not even figure in many sexual encounters. Add to this the lack of awareness of female sexuality and the sexual shaming that our culture reinforces. The *chhee-chhee-thoo-thoo* when it comes to any mention of breasts, nipples or vagina, the disgust associated with the female body is so entrenched that many women feel embarrassed to use the word 'vagina' even in private conversations with other women they are close to. 'Down there' is a territory many women allude to only when it is in extreme discomfort for some reason, and only by way of subtle gestures or code words. If women themselves can't even talk about their nether parts without worrying that they will offend someone, and without the burden of coyness and shame, how can they own the pleasure that their bodies are capable of making them feel? In the words of Germaine Greer, an Australian writer and one of the strongest voices in feminism, 'The cunt must come into its own.'

But, like Pradyum said, women aren't the only ones who struggle with sexual dysfunctions. 'Everyone assumes men are always having good sex, and enjoying it, when that's not the case,' he had pointed out. To understand more about this, I turn to Chandra. Sexual dysfunctions make for a big chunk of the cases he sees among men. He tells me that the three most common sexual dysfunctions among men in India are: premature ejaculation,[5] erectile dysfunction[6] and Dhat syndrome.[7]

Let's start with Dhat syndrome. I always — mistakenly — believed that Dhat syndrome is something that shows up among those who either aren't educated or are religious fanatics. Indeed, according to a 2019 study, illiteracy, age below twenty-four, marriage and living in rural areas are factors heavily associated with Dhat syndrome.[8] This is what I believed too — that it's something bred out of ignorance.

But Chandra points out something that stops me in my tracks. While telling me about Dhat syndrome, he mentions that many men avoid sex when they are following a demanding fitness regime because they fear they will lose energy. It's the same with masturbation; they avoid it because they don't want to lose out on 'vital' energy. This isn't something I personally haven't come across before. Gym instructors sometimes propagate this myth when they tell their male clients to abstain from sex or masturbation if they want to build muscle mass, because semen loss will lead to protein loss.

One man in his mid-thirties — educated and an atheist — mentioned in a casual conversation that he

[5] Premature ejaculation: When a man ejaculates in less than a minute of starting intercourse.

[6] Erectile dysfunction: The inability to maintain an erection.

[7] Dhat syndrome: Dhat syndrome is a culture-bound syndrome that leads to 'semen loss' related psychological distress. It is primarily seen in the Indian subcontinent but is prevalent in some other cultures as well. It emanates from the belief that the semen contains vital energy, and when expelled, it leads to loss of energy.

[8] Kuchal, Ashwini Kumar, Kumar, Saurav, Pardal, Pavan Kumar, Aggarwal, Gaurav, 'Effect of Dhat Syndrome on Body and Mind', *International Journal Of Contemporary Medical Research*, 2019

likes to have sex at night because he gets depleted of energy after it. He told me in a matter-of-fact fashion, 'Men get tired after sex. Women get energy.' I never questioned it. But after learning from Chandra how deeply the message that 'semen is vital energy' gets ingrained in men's psyche, I realized that he too had internalized this idea.

Both premature ejaculation and erectile dysfunction, Chandra tells me, are largely psychological. 'There is a lot of anxiety around sex. We grow up listening that sex is a sin, that it's something shameful. These messages leave an impact and later in life can cause problems,' he tells me.

Many of us learn about sex from watching porn, and while we know that pornography is doctored, we don't always understand just how much of it is unreliable. One such false learning men take from watching porn is that they are supposed to last a long time — twenty to thirty minutes. This leads many men to believe they have premature ejaculation when they actually don't. 'Whenever someone tells me they have premature ejaculation, the first thing I ask them is how long they last after penetration. Most of them tell me they last five to ten minutes. That's not premature ejaculation,' Chandra tells me. The normal range for men is between four minutes and thirty minutes. But because of lack of education, many men feel anything less than twenty minutes should raise alarm bells.

From mistakenly believing that there's something wrong with you, to getting help and having these myths dispelled is a long and complicated road, I'd imagine. I wonder how many men actually end up getting help or even voicing their concerns. I know for a fact that many women never get there; many internalize false and unrealistic ideas about sex. Many accept that sex is only a matter of duty, procreation and never about pleasure, and in silence, carry on. I wonder, then, if men who feel there's something wrong with them, suffer in silence too?

Chandra tells me men tend to avoid sex when they don't feel confident about themselves. Sounds familiar. Women do it too. When we don't feel attractive enough because of tummy rolls, body hair, cellulite and all the other things that make our bodies human. When a woman doesn't enjoy sex with someone, the first instinct for most is to find excuses. That mythical headache that has become the butt of many jokes.

Even in sex, then, men and women are more alike than not.

CHANGING THE SCRIPT

We tend to qualify and quantify sex based on an overt biological response — the orgasm. From start to finish, we chase the goal of climaxing. When we are unable to achieve this goal, it leads to disappointment and feelings of inadequacy. When women complain of not being able to orgasm, despite being in good health, they are told to not think about reaching climax and simply enjoy the process. The more we focus on reaching the goal, the harder it becomes to get there. Reframing sex as an interaction between two people, designed to make us feel good every step of the way, and not simply lead us to an explosive climax, can help relieve some of the anxiety around it. This interaction isn't simply limited to when you're in bed together. It's ongoing, and what you bring under the sheets is a cumulation of everything happening away from it. Unfortunately, in today's busy world, we're always rushing. There's always so much to do and it's almost impossible to slow down. The sex has become rushed too.

Thanks to smart phones and the Internet, the way we meet someone new, fall in love, have fights and have sex has changed remarkably. We can be in bed in crushed pyjamas and a bag of Doritos in one hand, and with the other, swipe right on the next person we end up with. Flirting has taken the form of sending memes and lifted the burden of being witty and romantic. And seduction…well, seduction has been reduced to dirty text messages and reluctant nudes. It's all high-speed and low effort.

We have paid the price with patience. We are becoming a generation for whom instant gratification is the norm. One can see this quick-fix craze in many things — ten-minute recipes, fast food outlets and quick workouts. When it comes to dating and relationships, it doesn't take long to download an app, upload a few attractive pictures, write a clever bio and swipe your way to a match. You may not find the one, but you will find someone to have a conversation with. But this swiftness of finding what your heart pleases is not the only thing that technology has impacted in the realm of relationships. The online world has given us access to more people than we have ever had or ever imagined. We are diving deep in a sea of options when it comes to matters of the heart!

Let me elucidate with a hypothetical situation: You get a match on a dating app. You chat, set up a date and meet. You spend a great couple of hours together and feel like you really click. But they refuse to take you home even though they may like to see you again. Now, if you are looking for sex — and you have another match waiting in your inbox — instead of focusing on this one person you clicked with, you can easily initiate a conversation with someone else and go get your carnal needs met. This happens commonly, and while you may not approve or may have been hurt by this, when it comes to casual sex, there is no real need to spend hours or days talking and getting to know each other. You may not have an intellectual or romantic connection with the one you indulge in casual sex with, but if it's mutual 'no-strings attached', then what is the problem? There is no need to 'waste' time.

But there is a need to seduce. There's always a need to seduce. The problem, however, is that seduction takes time and effort, and where we have options a swipe away and someone — or the hope that someone is there who won't need to be seduced beyond a drink or two — may be keeping us from investing in any one pursuit wholeheartedly.

Seduction is slow and deliberate. It benefits from anticipation and waiting. But the promptness of technology, combined with the ease of access that it offers, is making us too impatient for this art. Sex is fast becoming just another activity that we do.

It's not that seduction has gone out of the window completely. Even in this quick-fix dating culture, we do seduce. We do it when we dress up our profile with our best pictures and carefully chosen words or when we pick a fancy place for the first date over the neighbourhood dive. Seduction itself may not be dying, but it is becoming too hurried, and perhaps, a bit distant and superficial.

Not only has the amount of time and effort we spend on enticing someone reduced remarkably, we seem to have also forgotten that seduction is an ongoing process. It doesn't stop once you consummate, except, of course, in the specific case of a one-night stand. If you want to see someone again, you can't disappear in between dates or demonstrate complete lack of interest once the act of sex is done. Unless, of course, it is mutual. To invoke desire, and to maintain it, we need to keep working on it. The work entails two aspects — taking care of your state of mind, your manners and appearance; and staying present for the other.

Say you want to have sex tomorrow night. There are two ways you can make it happen in the scenario that you have a partner. One is: you wake up, go through your morning routine, get dressed, have breakfast, go to work, maybe do a quick check-in with your partner during your lunch break and get back to work. Closer to the evening, you maybe drop a text to let them know when you're coming home. You reach home, have dinner while you watch TV, and get into bed. You roll over and make your move.

In the second scenario, you wake up and give your partner a loving kiss on the cheek, or if they don't live with you, send them a text or call them to wish them good morning. Through the day, you send them a couple of pictures or maybe a joke or two or call during your lunch break to say hi. Closer to the evening, you reserve a table for two, or perhaps, decide to cook together at home or order in…it's a mutual decision. You head home to your partner and give them a peck as you enter. You step into the shower and scrub yourself clean. Then you arrange the meal together, filling each other in about your day, laughing, tuned out of the television or your phones and paying attention to each other, being present. All the while, you are being playful — a peck on the cheek every now and then, quick caresses on the small of the back while one pours the drinks. You finish dinner and get into bed and make your move.

In which case are you more likely to have a mutually satisfactory sexual experience?

As much as sexual satisfaction leads to overall relationship satisfaction, the opposite is true as well. This means that seduction is not merely about physical titillation or bringing flowers on the day you want to have sex, but rather an ongoing transaction that becomes an important part of the relationship. Its cornerstone is being present, whole. Seduction goes beyond pursuing a partner. It holds equal importance when it comes to maintaining the partnership. To think that seduction doesn't hold value in a long-term partnership is a folly many of us are guilty of and suffer by. This is why passion runs out, and instead of understanding that passion — a byproduct of seduction — is a fire we need to keep refuelling, we seek to seduce and be seduced by someone other than our partner. Passion ebbs and flows, yes, but when it dies, it is because we fail to understand that to keep it flowing, we need to be proactive.

Seduction is more than a sexual act. Seduction is sensual. It entices and awakens all the senses — our sense of smell with the perfumes we sprinkle ourselves with; our sense of sight with the clothes we adorn; our sense of taste with the food we offer and consume; our sense of hearing with the words we utter to each other; and finally, our sense of touch with how we caress each other's body. Seduction is also emotional and intellectual. Without connecting at these levels, you are not seducing — you are fucking.

Excess Baggage

'If I'm the only one she's been with, then I'm the best she's been with.'

— Ankit, twenty-nine

Even today in urban India, many people end up marrying their first love or the first person they've been sexually involved with. Many high school or college lovers later become spouses and then parents, whereas those who know that they will have to go through with an arranged marriage, avoid getting too attached to anyone. This idea that there is a 'the one' for all of us is reinforced in many ways. By not allowing opposite-sex friendships, we reinforce this idea that any intimate relationship between a male and a female must be romantic. Divorce is still a taboo. India has one of the lowest divorce rates globally, with only thirteen in 1,000 marriages ending in divorce.[9] When a couple expresses the desire to part ways, it often becomes a family affair, replete with interventions to save the dying marriage. This too reinforces the idea

[9] Menon, Rishika, 'Divorce and Remarriage: Still a Shame?', National School of Journalism and Public Disclosure, 8 May 2020

that when we commit to someone, we must honour it for eternity. There is a moral value attached with monogamy and life-term relationships. I use the term 'life-term' relationships to differentiate from long-term relationships. Many couples who are in a long-term relationship keep their relationship status a secret from family, colleagues and acquaintances until it becomes officially 'life-term'. It is only when the couple decides that they want to get married do they tell the family. Some, whose families are open-minded, may tell their parents, but the extended social circle only hears the news when there's a wedding in order. In our culture, we don't date for the sake of dating or to see if there is potential. Instead, we date to marry.

THE FOLLY OF 'THE ONE'

This idea that love and commitment is something that happens only once in a lifetime, and only with one person, is summed up the best by Shah Rukh Khan's famous dialogue from the blockbuster movie *Kuch Kuch Hota Hai*: '*Hum ek baar jeete hain, ek baar marte hain, shaadi bhi ek baar hoti hai, aur pyaar ek baar hi hota hai.*'

Growing up, Tushar was a die-hard Shah Rukh Khan fan. Tushar is the middle child, with an older brother and a younger sister. He grew up in Udaipur and moved to Mumbai when he turned eighteen to study engineering. The portrayal of love in the movies he grew up watching influenced his expectations of relationships. In his thirties now, he looks back at his naïveté with chagrin. 'I really did believe that's how love is — you meet the love of your life and then things are perfect. *She* is perfect,' he tells me over a WhatsApp video call. He's sitting in a park outside his home where he goes for his daily walks. Every now and then, he lowers his voice and looks over his shoulder to ensure he's not within anyone's earshot. Then he whispers with a crooked smile, 'My wife's not perfect.'

It's about more than perfection though. Having had more than one partner, or an active dating life is often frowned upon by 'Indian society'. There is a moral value and social sanction attached to life-term relationships, which makes everything else seem like excess baggage. We are made to believe that there is one person who is our 'soulmate'. That one person who is a perfect fit. When we are confronted with a partner's past, we are mortified at the possibility that we may not be 'the one' but a compromise. We tend to fill in the blanks with self-doubt and feel threatened by bygones. Romanticizing 'the one' doesn't serve anyone well. Being an ideal partner is not a function of some cosmic intervention but rather the result of both parties' effort. When a relationship fails it's because one of the two, or both, did not nurture the relationship whereas when both parties continuously and dedicatedly nurture the relationship, it usually lasts. If one must hold on to the idea of 'the one', it's important to remember then that anybody can be 'the one' as long as both of you are committed to making the relationship last.

This excess baggage also weighs differently for men and women. Society is generally more forgiving of men with a romantic or sexual past, and women, generally more accepting. A man who has had girlfriends before is accepted without much judgement or shame because we believe this is just how men are, and that 'men will be men'. A woman's past, though, is looked upon harshly and not without judgement. Among other things, for many men, it seems to invoke a host of insecurities. It seems to threaten the notion that in relationships, men take the lead.

Roshan is a thirty-four-year-old English teacher who moved to Delhi from Agra to escape his MLA father, who was deeply disappointed by his son's professional and sartorial choices. Roshan likes wearing pastel shirts and khaki pants, which was always a bone of contention between him and his crisp white kurta donning father. Roshan's refusal to enter politics was so unpalatable to his father that the two, as it stands, don't talk to each other anymore. Roshan and I settle on beanbags on the terrace of his humble *barsaati* behind Hauz Khas Village. His ex-girlfriend, Dyuti, painted a mural on the wall against which he has placed lush palms in red earthen pots.

After Dyuti moved to Germany for her masters, Roshan was once again single. Even though this thirty-something likes to date younger women, he has friends who are his age. One of his friends who's also touching forty set him up with the thirty-eight-year-old Manjari, a single mom to a teenage boy. 'It's very different from anything I've ever had before,' Roshan leans back into the bean bag, where we talk about his new lover over a cup of coffee. I ask him how so. 'The body,' he hesitates, looking for the right words. 'It's a mom's body…loose skin,' he pauses once again and finishes the thought with a 'yeah.'

We segue into the other aspects of his relationship with Manjari — how their date nights are determined by her schedule and not his whims. How he can't go over to her house because she doesn't want her son to meet him just yet. How she isn't 'open to trying' many things because she is set in her ways. 'Even simple things like — I'd take Dyuti on these camping trips and make her have these new experiences. Manjari has done all of it or she's not interested. I don't know if that's a personality thing or if it's the age.'

'So she's more in control of the relationship?' I ask.

'That's one way to put it. I think on the physical side too — she knows what she wants. That's a good thing, but sometimes, I feel she wants me to do only those things her ex-husband did with her.' I note how in Roshan's mind, Manjari's sexuality is directed by a man — her ex-husband.

He doesn't think the relationship will last. He's too used to being with women with little to no experience in love and sex. He prefers that. 'I become the benchmark for women who've not had boyfriends before me. I like that feeling. I like knowing that wherever they go after here, I will always be the guy they can't match up to.'

MEN ARE COLLECTORS

I met Dushyant at a party thrown by a mutual friend. Affable and charming, he and I struck up a conversation, flirting and laughing while enjoying the music. Later, my friend told me she thinks he's 'scatter-brained'. Over the next few months, I would run into Dushyant several times. Each time, he'd have company. Each time, a different woman. One evening, as a few of us — me, Dushyant and our mutual friends — huddled around a table at a bar, a young woman walked over and introduced herself to us. 'Hi, I'm Dushyant's girlfriend's best friend,' she declared. Dushyant smirked at us and told us her name. And then, to her, 'We're just hanging out.'

None of us at the table knew Dushyant had a girlfriend. We'd always seen him bring a different date to every party, every evening out and had assumed he was casually dating or hooking up. As soon as his girlfriend's best friend was out of earshot, we jumped at him. 'She's in the UK,' he told us. We asked him about the women he brought to our evenings out. Were they in an open relationship? Did she know about his dalliances? After trying to deflect the questions with jokes a few times, he finally said, 'I want a harem. But I want to be the only guy in a woman's life.' He then laughed, trying to pass off the statement as another joke. Like his watches and leather shoes, Dushyant wanted a collection of women. Dushyant isn't the only man in his twenties who wants to be a king with a 'harem' of concubines.

He tells us that he's not ready to be monogamous yet. That he loves his girlfriend and wants to marry her one day, but for now, he wants to 'have fun and explore'. But he also wants to be the only man in these women's lives. So fun and exploration for him alone, not for the women.

I wonder if this fantasy of having a 'harem' is a disastrous byproduct of men's conditioning to acquire things, and social structures that treat women as 'things'. Men are collectors. They buy gadgets they don't really need, adorn watches that cost more than the monthly income of the majority of the country's population, and treat their cars as status symbols. As we have seen, men across all ages tend to treat women (girlfriends, wives, escorts or a harem) as trophies that elevate their status in some way. To many men, women continue to be possessions, even if these men may not be controlling or possessive or otherwise abusive.

This attitude of treating women as objects of fun, exploration and experimentation, is also reinforced by our culture. Let's consider how we view male and female virginity. Whereas a woman's virginity is an eligibility criterion in marriage, for a young man, losing his virginity is a rite of passage into manhood. The very fact that we have female sex workers who cater to virgin boys and no equivalent of this for women, is another example of how our society encourages sexual proclivity among men, not women. Male virginity is neither a symbol of character nor a badge of honour. Contrary to young girls whose sexuality is systematically curtailed, young boys openly flirt with girls and try to woo them. They are encouraged to have many girlfriends as a display of their budding manhood. Not much is made of an adolescent boy or a young adult man with multiple flings or relationships. A man who is popular among women is usually admired by his male companions. The worst onslaught he receives is being labelled a 'lady's man', 'stud' or 'player'...nothing as damaging as a woman who might be labelled a 'whore', 'slut', 'characterless' or shunned away as 'not marriage material'. While for a young man, it is almost a matter of pride to have had many lovers, for a young woman it is a matter of shame. Indeed, a woman's character is demonstrated by her loyalty to 'the one', even if she may not have come across him yet, while a man's character is demonstrated by how many women he can sway.

So if the charming, witty, well-spoken, well-dressed and successful Dushyant isn't a modern, urban version of this, then what is his harem fantasy about?

STUCK IN THE MIDDLE WITH YOU

For twenty-nine-year-old Ankit, knowing that his to-be wife has never been with anyone else brings him 'mental peace'. 'If I'm the only one she's been with, then I'm the best she's been with,' he tells me. 'She won't have anything to compare me to so that's a good thing for sure.' Ankit has had girlfriends in the past. He has been sexually involved with one, so he certainly has someone to compare his wife to. To him, though, it's not the same. 'One of us should know what to do,' he laughs.

When I asked men if they preferred being with a virgin, most of the responses I received ranged between: 'yes' to 'no, but I don't want someone with too much sexual experience either'. The reasons ranged from: 'A virgin won't have anything to compare me against' to 'I don't want a virgin because it's messy and virgins get attached'. So for casual sex, men seem to prefer women who are already sexually active, while those looking for a serious relationship are more comfortable with a woman who hasn't had too many lovers before.

For some of the young men I spoke to, virginity is no longer a matter of morality. Many men in urban India seem to have broken out of that conditioning, as have the women. Those in their twenties and thirties today don't see sex only as a tool of procreation reserved for after marriage. We have broken out of that paradigm and see sex as a necessary part of a relationship.

But a partner's sexual and romantic past continues to be a source of discomfort and a trigger for insecurities. When one is jealous of a partner's ex, it is called 'retroactive jealousy'. Research shows that retroactive jealousy is exacerbated by social media — those pictures that weren't deleted or the way social media makes it easy to keep tabs on a partner's ex.[1] Chandra tells me that how a man responds to his partner's past largely depends on how she speaks about it. 'If she draws comparisons between her ex and her current partner, he is bound to feel insecure. And this isn't true only for sex. This is equally true for how he looks, his financial status and so on.'

A woman's virginity has been a long-standing obsession in our country. But today, India is at a cusp. The youth today are caught between patriarchal family structures and a sexual revolution. This conflict makes itself apparent in the values we attach to sex. According to a survey published in *Hindustan Times*, 61 per cent of the country's youth no longer frown upon premarital sex. But the same survey also reveals that 63 per cent want to marry a virgin![2]

On the one hand, many of us are discarding old value systems and exploring our sexualities but when it comes

[1] Frampton, Jessica R., Fox, Jesse, 'Social Media's Role In Romantic Partners' Retroactive Jealousy: Social Comparison, Uncertainty and Information Seeking', SAGE, 2018

[2] Bawa, Jyoti Sharma, '63% Want to Marry Virgins, But Majority Approve of Premarital Sex', *Hindustan Times*, 3 September 2015

to life-term commitment, we still rely on the 'wisdom' of the generations before us who are orthodox in their opinions on sexuality and love. Modern India is more progressive in their thought, but it seems mostly only at a thought level. We haven't yet reached that stage in this cultural transformation where these thoughts are freely manifested.

A 2016 survey of over 6,000 individuals between the ages fifteen and thirty-four revealed that 50 per cent of the respondents would prefer arranged marriage. Those who prefered love marriage comprised only 12 per cent of the people in this survey![3] One of the criteria for an *adarsh bahu* (ideal daughter-in-law) is that she should not have had too many lovers and our preference for this system reflects that at some level we trust it.

Virginity, then, is not just sexual. There is also what I call 'love virginity'. A woman who has had only one partner all her life is believed to have a sense of stability and maturity. A woman who has had multiple lovers is quick to be judged and her character slammed. On rare occasions, a man may be considered unfit for marriage or a relationship, but seldom is he put through the kind of shaming and scrutiny like a woman with a past. Patriarchy puts a premium on the sexual prowess of men. If so many men believe that women are 'achievements' then it only makes sense that she must not be hand-me-down. Just like a second-hand car, a woman who's been previously loved seems to have less value. Her honour, character and worth are tied to her love life and saved for the man who weds her.

[3] Sampath, G., 'Indian Youth Look Modern But Inclined To Conservatism And Intolerance: Survey', *The Hindu*, 5 April, 2017

The hunt for a virgin bride impacts more than just the sexual maps of women and men. More than a quarter of young men and women today are having sex before marriage.[4] Casual sex is no longer frowned upon. The advent of dating apps has given birth to 'hook up' culture wherein it is becoming acceptable for a woman, or a man, to say they're in it for the sex. Yet the ripple effects of attaching moral value to both sexual and 'love virginity' are seen in modern relationships.

Often, young men who openly talk about their past get uncomfortable when the woman talks about hers. They put on blinders.

Twenty-seven-year-old Manav married the second woman he was ever involved with, barring a few drunken make-out sessions here and there. 'My wife has had an interesting sex life. She had a threesome in college with her friend and her boyfriend. She told me when we were dating. It was weird for me to listen to that. So I told her I didn't want to know. Otherwise, we have a good sex life. I sometimes wonder if she compares me with her exes. But I don't want to know.'

This is a common sentiment among many men today: They are okay with a partner's sexual history as long as it's not more colourful than their own, and as long as they don't know the details.

Ours is perhaps the first generation in India that is embracing casual dating, and while this is breaking apart some of the social structures that elevated virginity and

---

[4] Sharma, Rohit, 'More Than A Quarter Of India's Youngsters Have Premarital Sex', *BMJ Open Access*, US National Public Library Of Medicine, 2001

life-term relationships to a superior status, it is also bringing with it a host of new problems.

With so many young men and women caught between the old philosophy of 'the one' and the new of 'anyone' who's available, we are learning to turn a blind eye to the others. Men, when confronted with a partner's ex-boyfriend or former FWB or fling or anything in between simply don't want to know.

Rachit tells me that his girlfriend's past doesn't matter to him. They don't talk about it much, and to him, that seems to be a non-issue. 'It's unnecessary to talk about bygones.' I ask him if he knows what happened or why they broke up. He tells me he doesn't and that whenever his girlfriend brings up the topic, he feels uncomfortable. Why? I ask. 'I don't know...' he shrugs. 'It's a little weird to imagine her with another guy.'

While reminiscing about a former lover, it occurred to me that he never really stopped keeping in touch with any of his exes. In fact, he would often hang out with his ex-girlfriends and current girlfriend at the same time. I first met him at a party where one of his exes was present. I saw pictures of him with the girl he dated after me and the one he dated before me partying together on several occasions. He's not the only man I've known who somehow manages to facilitate harmony between a former and a present love interest. But when it comes to developing a cordial relationship with their girlfriend's ex, the same men become awkward and insecure. It's not that they judge the ex or the woman for having a past. For men like him, it's not a moral issue but rather the fear that he may not be able to match up to the ex. It's an instinctive need to protect their territory.

We're neither here nor there.

THE PAST MAKES THE FUTURE

Men seem to be okay having multiple partners themselves but also have a deep desire to obliterate a woman's past. By putting on blinders, men tell women that they wished this part — or past — of hers didn't exist.

This is a slippery slope.

It robs a relationship of its authenticity. No one is obliged to talk about the details of their past. But when a subject becomes taboo the relationship can become calculated. When men judge women for their past or feel uncomfortable and awkward when an ex-boyfriend comes up in conversation, it makes the woman hold back. Like men become self-conscious when their partner talks about an ex in a positive light, or compares them to an ex, women feel the same when they get taunted for having a past.

One must not forget that every relationship is a learning experience. With every dalliance, fling, lustful adventure and heartfelt love, we learn something about others, about relationships, and most importantly, about our own selves. Of course, some people don't learn from their experiences. But, those who embrace life as a learning experience will have put themselves out there, sought adventures and misadventures that help them grow. That person is invaluable. We understand this about human nature when it comes to education, travel and work. But in relationships, it seems we have an entirely different rulebook. Instead of trying to understand the person with the list of erstwhile partners, we stereotype them without giving them a chance.

Women who have dated more than one or two men are often slut shamed. It's not unheard of to assume that a woman who's had several boyfriends will not be loyal to anyone. But the past is not always a fair measure when it comes to relationships.

Sonal tells me, 'I was only twenty-two when I got married. What did I even know about the world? It was an arranged marriage. Good family, successful…all that bullshit. So I did it. But it was always a loveless marriage. I am happy now.' She smiles at me and walks to the kitchen in her one-bedroom apartment in a posh Delhi neighbourhood. As she brews two cups of chamomile tea, she tells me about the first time a man other than her ex-husband showered her with attention. 'It was so thrilling. I had never felt that way. I never thought I would, you know. My ex-husband would not even look at me. Sex, which, by the way, was rare with him, was so…mechanical. But this guy opened up a whole new world for me, and I saw what I had been missing out on.' She clarifies, 'My husband didn't know about Vikas until after the divorce came through. And even then, he wanted to keep up the appearances. You know how it is in these circles, right. But I refused to live a half-life anymore. I am no longer with Vikas. I am single right now. Maybe I'll find someone when I am ready. But at least now I know what I want, which I didn't as an inexperienced twenty-two-year-old.' Here's a woman who was married off as a virgin with no previous boyfriends and yet she cheated. Or perhaps that's why. Infidelity is complex and multi-layered and to pin it on one thing alone is short-sighted and ill-informed.

All said and done, it can be unnerving to confront a partner's romantic or sexual past. It can lead to all sorts of doubts and insecurities. What if she is still emotionally attached to her ex? Is there something she is hiding from me? Was it her fault that the relationship ended? What if I never match up? What if she doesn't open up to me like how she did with her ex? What if I'm a compromise?

Archit had these concerns too. He is thirty-two years old and in love with Shruti, who is three years older than him and divorced. They met on a vacation and hit it off. While Shruti works in Gurugram, Archit runs a production house in the heart of Delhi. Shruti lives with her parents, and Archit lives with two flat mates. They've been together for a little over two years. 'I took it really slow in the beginning. I had some doubts. I wanted to know what happened with her ex, but I also didn't,' he laughs. 'It's hard to hear all this, man. But I knew it was important for me to understand where she came from. If I was serious about this relationship. And the more I heard about her past, I realized why she is the way she is now — so guarded and she doesn't tolerate some things in the relationship. So I understand now.' He tells me about Shruti's little quirks with a twinkle in his eye and awe in his voice. He's full of praise for her. 'She's so bright and so good at her work. I'm so proud of her. And she's so nice to my friends. She's a star,' he tells me. 'I do think what happened with her has made her stronger...and more patient.'

Most people get better at relationships as they grow older and gain more experience. Many women I know, who've dated some questionable men during their twenties and found healthier ways of loving and being loved later in life, testify that they appreciate a nurturing partner and relationship now a lot more than they did a decade ago because of the bad experiences.

The premium put on a woman's chastity also strips men of a sense of privacy and the freedom to choose the woman they would like to be with. What if a man from a community or tribe where only a virgin is considered good enough to be a wife finds himself in love with someone who has had past sexual experience? What if an urban man from an orthodox family finds himself in love with someone who's previously been married? Should he have to justify his desire to himself and 'society'? Unfortunately, in the society that we live in, the answer is usually yes.

Archit told his parents about Shruti only six months ago. He knew they wouldn't be happy that he's dating someone who's divorced. He was right. 'My father didn't talk to me for a month,' he tells me. Archit is from Kanpur. His mother, he tells me, has a 'mischievous mind'. She would tease him about girls when he was a teenager. 'But when I told her about my first girlfriend, my mother said, "*Papa ko nahi bataana* (don't tell your father)". My dad is old-fashioned. He still thinks you should not have girlfriends and get married straightaway. But to someone who has also never had any boyfriends in the past. That is important to him. So imagine how angry he must be about this.'

It is exactly this rigid attitude that Archit strives to get away from. 'I want to be as far away from that as possible. It's not right to treat women like this. My mother had a tough life because of attitudes like this. I want to give my wife, or girlfriend, the respect she deserves.'

There are no generalizations; only individuals trying to navigate this paradigm shift we are going through.

PART THREE

Dating

Online Dating

'I feel good when I do it [ghosting] to someone. I feel like, yes, I can also do this.'

— Karthik, thirty-four

'Is this Prachi?' The gentleman on the other end of the line said.

I responded in the affirmative.

'I'm Rahul. I saw your profile on Tinder and I was really impressed by what I saw,' he said.

I responded with silence, the awkwardness of which was palpable through the phone.

'But don't think that I just saw your pictures and decided to call you. I actually researched you. You are a writer...you do yoga. I was quite impressed, and I just wanted to talk to you.' Confused, I asked him to explain, and he told me that he had swiped right on my profile on Tinder and when we didn't match, he took the pains of searching for my contact information on Google. All because he liked my pictures and a half-hearted two-liner bio.

At this point, I told him, as politely as I could, that him looking me up on Google, finding out more than I'd let out on my dating profile, was not the act of niceness he thought it was. That just because my number is available on the internet doesn't mean one can call and chat me up and that he should not try to contact me again.

Rahul apologized and never tried to contact me again, which I deeply appreciate. I am compelled to give him the benefit of the doubt and assume that he was acting from a place of ignorance rather than entitlement. But not all men act like that. Ask any woman who has used a dating app and she will happily share with you her inbox full of unsolicited messages from men she did not swipe right on but who found a way to reach out to her nonetheless.

What makes a man reach out to a stranger online?

'It's really not a big deal, bro. Every platform is a dating app,' twenty-four-year-old Shashwat tells me. I ask him to explain what he means. 'See, if I match with someone on a dating app, that doesn't mean she's my girlfriend now. It means we chat and if we like chatting with each other, we meet. And it goes on from there. So what difference does it make whether we chat on Hinge or Instagram? Or if I email or Google her? It's all the same. Anyway, it's so easy to find out all the information about someone online these days.'

I can't retort. I am reminded of an interview I once conducted with Taru Gupta, General Manager, Tinder India, during which she had told me the same thing. 'Tinder is simply an introduction platform. We don't influence what happens after a match is made.'

People have been meeting strangers on the internet, and falling in love, since before the surge of online dating apps. Before applications that are tailored to facilitating romance and sexual encounters we had Yahoo chat rooms and Orkut. Both platforms were popular meet-up portals for those who were single and ready to mingle.

Tushar met his wife in a Yahoo chat room. For around six months, they chatted online, emailed pictures to each other and Skyped. One lived in Agra, the other in Pune, yet they fell in love through a screen. This was not unheard of back in the day of Yahoo chat rooms that were categorized by location and interest. For example, 'Dilli dilwalon ki', 'FRIENDS fan club', 'Music lovers'. Then there were rooms dedicated to people who wanted to flirt or meet someone new. Some rooms had some not safe for work (NSFW) activities going on too. In some ways, Yahoo chat rooms were wilder than the predictable, vanilla, regulated dating apps of today.

Also, perhaps, much less safe. But then cyber security wasn't a big concern in the early days of digitization. There was also no way to verify the person's identity, to filter by interests (as is now possible on several apps like OkCupid) or to make a profile on which one could offer a short introduction about themselves. All these features were missing from the infamous chat rooms. Like the honeymoon phase of relationships, we were romancing the internet, giving it a chance, a chink in the window, without realizing it would barge in with full gusto and change the interiors of our homes beyond recognition.

ONLINE DATING — A PARADIGM SHIFT

While it wasn't impossible to meet strangers online before dating apps came about, it was still under wraps and considered to be somewhat of an oddity. One did it on the sly. Embracing online dating as a legitimate way of meeting people has brought with it a paradigm shift. It has opened a fascinating world of casual sex, FWB, almost-relationships, dating for the sake of dating, and for the hopeless romantics, finding the love of one's life on one's own terms. It has made it possible to overcome false social boundaries created by our insular social structures and maintained by our comfort with the familiar. The Internet enables meeting people who come from a different world. Thanks to the plethora of dating applications available to us, the door is now open to many experiences — from having a cup of coffee with the cute boy/girl next door to a Bollywood movie marathon with an eager expat to dinner and drinks that culminates in mind-blowing sex and a series of dates that end up as accidental love!

Tinder — one of the most popular dating applications globally — launched in India in 2016. From hopeful singles to the recently broken up, nearly everyone was on it, at least in the metropolis. Popularized as a hook-up app, Tinder became the new avenue to meet people and create all sorts of alliances. The app's success brought along more dating apps — Bumble, Truly Madly, Happn, Hinge, etc., each with its unique features. In recent years, we have also seen more niche online dating services. There is a surge of dating or matchmaking apps that cater to specific groups — Aisle for Indians across the globe, AndWeMet for urban Indians over thirty, ReKindle for those who've been previously married.

In 2021, online dating is no longer a big-city thing. It is fast gaining popularity in tier two and three cities as well.

To some men the world of online dating apps has come as a sigh of relief. Twenty-nine year old Angad is an introvert. He has a small circle of three close friends with whom he likes to hang out, and is never seen at parties. He's never been comfortable with chatting up an attractive woman at a pub or a cafe, or even a gathering with mutual friends. For him, dating apps are a respite. 'When it's a text message, it's okay if she doesn't respond. But imagine saying hi to a cute girl at a bar and she turns around and walks off! How embarrassing would that be!,' he tells me.

Striking a conversation behind the safety of one's smartphone not only protects us from such embarrassment, it also helps make a good first impression. The same can be said for women. In fact, for women, dating apps have helped in normalizing making the first move. Technology allows us to surpass the barrier of social inhibitions. A match might not always go where you wanted it to, but rejection hurts less in the virtual world.

During the pandemic, when social distancing has become a survival skill, dating apps and online video chats provide relief from isolation for many. In an article published by *Forbes*, CEOs, VPs and spokespersons of various popular dating apps shared that during the lockdown, people spent more time on dating apps. Bumble users were also 38 per cent more likely to have video chats with their dates.[1]

Some women feel safer in the pandemic-driven dating diaspora where meeting per convenience is

---

[1] Shetty, Aishwarya, 'How Homegrown Dating Apps are Finding Love in India', *Forbes India*, 30 December 2020

not possible, and they have to resort to video chats to get to know the person on the other side of the phone. Varnika is thirty-one and lives in Delhi with her parents. She is a financial advisor who, before the pandemic, would travel often for both work and leisure. She tells me, 'It's actually been a blessing. I have a couple of matches, and I've had quite a few video dates with each of them. I have a preference already without meeting either of them. It's also helped me feel safe…there's already some level of trust with this one guy.'

It's interesting to note that while video chats have been available to us for quite a few years now, seldom has anyone, who could meet their match in person, thought of using video chats as a way to vet them. I suppose despite how easy technology has made it to get to know someone without really meeting them, we want to hold on to that element of mystery and surprise. Even though we can access information about a match online, we want to experience that moment of novelty and surprise when we finally meet them. We want to meet them as if they were a stranger we met while out on a leisurely walk.

EVERY ROSE HAS ITS THORN

Aadil uses Hinge, Tinder and Bumble, and has had dates that have ranged from 'amazing' to 'horrendous'. With his family in Kolkata, he found himself alone during the lockdown. He had nowhere to go and thus was spending more time swiping left and right on dating apps. The number of matches he had and the people he was chatting with increased dramatically.

'It was not about dating during that time,' he tells me. 'Everybody just needed someone to talk to. You're bored. You open your matches and start chatting with someone. It wasn't about hooking up or anything like that.' The time he refers to is between March and May 2020. During those months, he was also left to cook for himself. 'So I was telling this one girl I'm living on toast and boiled eggs because my cook is not coming and she taught me these amazing chicken recipes on video. That was nice.'

What about the 'horrendous' online dating experiences? For Aadil, the most horrifying experience was discovering the world of married women looking for casual hookups online. 'I didn't know this was so common. There are so many women in their thirties who are married but use dating apps for hook ups.' While Aadil is not keen on becoming a married woman's lover, he did meet one who claimed her husband didn't live in Delhi and he knew she was using these apps. They married young and she wanted to explore. The husband was okay with it. 'But it was just weird.' Aadil cringes as he reminisces about his only date with the woman. 'First, she said she couldn't get out at night because she lives with her in-laws. Then she didn't want to go out to a public place. She just wanted to meet at home. It was just not my thing.'

For Peeyush Pandey, the struggles fall on the opposite end of the spectrum. Recently turned twenty-five and busy with work, he is not looking for anything serious. The age bracket he's set for profile suggestions on the app is within a couple of years of his own. 'But most women are looking for something serious. I think age is a factor.' I ask him how he knows most women are looking for something serious, naively assuming one wouldn't mention 'looking for commitment' on their profile. 'They write it in their bio,' he tells me, crushing my ignorance. 'Or they tell you in the first few interactions.' But he tells me he has had more success with dating apps when he was in Bengaluru. He moved to Gurugram a little over a year ago and is still nostalgic about how much easier casual dating was in Bengaluru. 'People are a lot more open there.'

A Tinder user in Delhi and Gurugram and a Hinge user in Bengaluru, Peeyush is of the opinion that there are many fake profiles on Tinder or people who don't reply or chat with you. The crowd on Hinge is friendlier. Peeyush isn't the only one who thinks Tinder is on its way out. Aadil, too, had met his gourmet chef on Hinge.

Online dating apps brought with them not only romantic possibilities but also a plethora of toxic trends. As a writer covering sex and relationships, I have to regularly update my lexicon of modern love and betrayal. My internal monologues sometimes sound like this: *NSA sex is often followed by ghosting.*[2] *While people experiment with throupling*[3] *and cuffing,*[4]

---

[2] Ghosting: Disappearing on someone without an explanation.

[3] Throupling/Throuple: A relationship between three people.

[4] Cuffing: The tendency of people to want to couple up during the cooler months — October through March. Although this is a borrowed concept from colder countries, one can see its parallel in India. October through February/March is festive and wedding season here and coupling up tends to increase during this time.

they also breadcrumb[5] *and have benchees.*[6] *Fleabaggers*[7] *are often submarined.*[8] *Should you white claw*[9] *or yellow card*[10] *that attractive but uninteresting and ignorant person you're dating these days? Gosh, I hope he's not a wokefish!*[11]

When a woman matches with a man on a dating app, she will search for him on Google. She will find his Facebook profile and peruse the pictures and posts that are public. She is relieved if she has mutual friends with this person. She will look for his Twitter feed, and of course, find him on Instagram. She wants to know how real he is and wants a glimpse of the kind of a life he lives. Women do this because we fear that the person on the other side of the screen may be a pervert, molester, stalker, a rapist, a killer. We want to know as much as we can before we let this person near us. We want to know that the person we will have coffee or drinks or dinner with is not a creep! Creep-quotient is the first screening. Once a woman has determined the guy on the other end is a decent human being, she wants to know if he's authentic. If he actually

---

[5] Breadcrumbing: Sending out just enough romantic or flirtatious signals to keep someone on the hook but being non-committal while you do so.

[6] Benching: When you hold someone on the back burner, maybe have a chat with them occasionally, see them once in a couple of weeks, all the while looking for other options, you are benching them. A benchee is your back-up plan.

[7] Fleabagging: Named after the popular British show Fleabag, this refers to the pattern of falling for people who are unavailable. It's based on actress Phoebe Waller-Bridge's character and how she navigates relationships.

[8] Submarining: This is when someone goes off the radar for some time, only to resurface later. What makes this awful is that when they do wriggle their way back into your life, they pretend like they never really made themselves unavailable.

[9] White clawing: Staying with someone you find attractive but otherwise uninteresting.

[10] Yellow card: To call out someone's bad behaviour.

[11] Wokefish: Pretending to be 'woke' or liberal to get someone's approval. From catfishing: pretending to be someone you're not.

believes in the liberal, pro-women statements he is making. So when a woman stalks a match online, she's also safeguarding herself against potential 'wokefishing'. Though one's online presence can be deceptive, one can still pick up cues, and if done smartly, these pieces put together do paint a sketch.

Peeyush agrees. He's worried about being catfished, not wokefished. 'I've heard many stories where people for like six months, eight months or years, have believed that this person they were talking to is someone else.' Because of these stories, Peeyush safeguards himself by using 'verification tactics'. 'So I ask them if we can chat on WhatsApp or you can look at their profile and the way they talk. Mostly, you can tell by that. If you don't pay attention to these subtle things, that's when you get trapped into this.'

What happens once you've done your background check and started talking to your match? Are there any common trends that affect almost everyone in the online dating pool at some point? The answer is yes. If there's one online dating trend almost everyone has either been subject to, or put someone else through, it is ghosting.

I ask Peeyush if he's ever been ghosted or has ghosted someone. He says yes to both, but thinks ghosting is fine if you've just matched or just started talking and don't feel that spark or attraction. He's ghosted a few women because of this. 'But if you've been talking for a while and maybe you've met also, and after that you ghost, that's annoying,' he adds.

Ghosting and relationships go hand in hand. Before this nomenclature, it was called 'abandonment'. Spousal abandonment is a widely accepted ground for divorce. Abandonment, in general, is seen as a copout in relationships, and it is indeed disrespectful and humiliating. But we are more forgiving of ghosting. Perhaps that demarcation that Peeyush points out is important — at what stage does one ghost?

For Karthik, though, ghosting is a way of reclaiming power. He is not an advocate of monogamy. But, he is married. Karthik sees sex as separate from love and commitment. Living in a separate city from his wife, he is active on dating apps and has been ghosted by, and ghosted, a few. 'It's like...I feel good when I do it to someone. I feel like, yes, I can also do this.' He puts his right hand in a fist and makes the winning gesture a cricketer makes when he hits a century.

Another common complaint that men have is that they don't get as many matches as women.

For thirty-year-old Jacob, online dating apps didn't work out well at all. 'I tried them, but it was not for me,' he tells me in his heavy Kannada accent. 'Once or twice, I met someone for coffee but the girls were just... we were not connecting.' Jacob has a gentle demeanour. Even as he talks about his disappointments with online dating apps — something his friends have had a lot of success with, he tells me — he has a hint of a smile on his face and serenity in his voice.

Some men indiscriminately swipe right on profiles, assuming they will match with only a few. Twenty-three-year-old Aayan tells me that he swipes right on 'pretty much every profile because guys anyway don't get as many matches as girls do. *Aise kisi se toh match ho jaayega.* (If I swipe right on all the profiles I like, at least I'll match with *someone.*)' He has had some luck with this strategy. But sometimes, after matching with someone, the conversation runs dry. 'One of the most annoying things is when you're chatting with someone and they reply in monosyllabes — hmm, ya, no. I'd never want to meet someone who acts like that. I want to feel some excitement — that you're excited to see me,' he says.

Online dating requires deftness and a whole lot of patience. One can't blindly swipe and meet, hoping to be infatuated by every match. On the contrary, for some, online dating is a rabbit hole of disappointments.

This is another irony of online dating. It has given us control over who we meet while also robbing us of control over who we speak to.

For divorced men in urban India — particularly in Mumbai — as I learnt, the thorn in online dating is sharper. Abhishek Kashyap is the founder of Rekindle — a dating app solely for previously married individuals. His pre-launch market research revealed that young, working women in Mumbai aren't interested in dating someone who has been previously married, while young men were more open to it. 'Men, whether they have been previously married or not, are looking for the same things — either long-term relationships or hook ups,' Abhishek tells me. 'Previously married men complain about being an outcast. They want to be a part of the dating pool. They want to be able to date whomever they want, but sadly that's not the case.' He tells me he didn't do enough research on why this was, but we ponder the reasons nonetheless.

Abhishek: 'I think subconsciously women think — I'm a single woman, I'm doing well in my life, why should I hang around with someone who might carry emotional baggage? The choice between a successful divorced thirty-year-old guy and a successful single guy (previously unmarried) becomes pretty obvious to a woman.'

Me: 'I'd guess that women probably don't want to deal with baggage. It is complicated because men and women deal with past relationships differently. I've learnt that men tend to hold on to their exes, even if it's as platonic friends. Men like to have their exes around. Whereas women generally tend to let go and completely cut off from their exes. Men like to foster friendships with their exes. I wonder if that's a factor?'

Abhishek: 'I think women become indifferent really quickly as compared to men. So yeah, I think you might be right.'

Me: 'I think it's a coping mechanism — a solution-focused decision that women make — rather than indifference. They cut off to simplify their lives. It's not that they have become indifferent to their exes. They just don't want the complications that could arise from having their exes around. They don't want that noise in their lives.'

Abhishek: 'If that's true, I think that's wonderful. I think men should have that.'

IN THE END, WE ARE HUMAN BEINGS ON A TECHNOLOGICAL JOURNEY

Using a service to find a partner is not a new concept. For generations now, we have relied on more than just our friends and families to meet potential suitors. From newspaper ads to matrimonial websites like *jeevansathi.com*, we have tried to transcend our immediate social circles, and *their* immediate social circles, to find 'the one'. Taking this search for a partner online has, quite literally, opened the whole world to us! Some research suggests that there has been a rise in interracial marriages because of the ease of access provided by digital platforms.[1] These platforms are a cultural melting pot and have enabled us to break out of our limiting social circles, and that is truly mind-blowing when you think about how it can potentially mould cultural diversity and unification in the future. Even so, the romantics believe that a picture and a short bio are not enough to fall in love. They are not, of course. And they aren't meant to be magic wands that connect people with their soulmates. These apps simply connect strangers; the rest is up to us.

That being said, the surge of online dating and the accompanying toxic trends have made some people wonder if the ease of access and lack of accountability is turning us into monsters. Trends such as catfishing, benching, submarining are a direct result of online dating. There are certainly many 'horror stories' out there but are they really a modern phenomenon or simply age-old human stories that have been repackaged and relabelled with a modern lingo?

Let's take infidelity as an example. Some believe that the Internet is making people less faithful. Aadil has certainly had his fair share of encounters with married women who are looking for something on the side. Many women in my circle have gone on dates with men they met online, who later told them they were married.

---

[1] Hergovich, Philipp, Ortega, Josue, 'The Strength of Absent Ties: Social Integration via Online Dating', Cornell University Open Access Library, 2017

There are subreddits (unabashedly called r/Affairs, r/OnlineAffairs) dedicated to people looking to have affairs. Then there are platforms such as Gleeden that promise 'discreet encounters'. The members are mostly married or in long-term relationships.

A few years ago, I got a call from the PR agent of one such platform for married individuals looking to meet new people. I was in the middle of filing a story and didn't have time for politeness. Abrasively, I told the agent I didn't want to know more as I wouldn't do a collaboration with a platform that promotes affairs. 'No, no. It's not for affairs,' he protested. 'It's for married people who are looking to meet new people — friendships.' I rolled my eyes at that trite pitch I'd heard from everyone associated with a dating app. 'I'm not interested,' I said one more time. He continued to persuade me until I snapped at him. I said something to the effect of, 'You think people are stupid? That if you say it's for friendships, people will believe you? We all know you're encouraging people to have affairs.' Poor guy. He was just doing his job (if you're reading this, I apologize).

Now older and wiser, I realize that it's not that the internet is making people less faithful; it is that those who are inclined towards infidelity now find it easier to cheat. Those who want to cheat will do so regardless of how you met them or whether they have access to online dating apps or not. And those who are loyal will remain so no matter how many dating apps you tempt them with. Technology can't change who you are. It can, however, make it easier for us to be more of who we are — frivolous or committed. Those looking for casual encounters now have a massive pool of people just a click away to choose from. As do the ones looking for commitment. This accessibility is one of the biggest changes that online dating has brought. Contrary to popular belief, there is no significant difference between the quality of a relationship formed with someone offline versus someone one met online, although relationships that start offline are more likely to progress to marriage.[2] A study conducted by researchers from the University of Chicago, Gestalt Researchers and Harvard, that surveyed over 19,000 couples across the United States who tied the knot between the years 2005 and 2012, found that those who met online reported a slight but significant higher satisfaction in their marriage. Divorce rates were also slightly lower among those who met their spouse online.[3]

Having said that, this technological journey we are on isn't smooth sailing. While it's magical to be able to talk to someone you otherwise never would have crossed paths with, dating apps have also brought us face-to-face with the 'paradox of choice'.

At one point, Aadil was chatting with six different women. There were days when he would have lunch with one, drinks with another, dinner with a third. 'They were all nice women...but nobody made me go like "wow! I just want to talk to this person and no one else". Then with time, I realized I wasn't feeling that for anyone I met. On paper, there were some women who

---

[2] Paul, Aditi, Is Online Better Than Offline For Meeting Partners? Depends: Are You Looking to Marry or Date?', *Cyberpsychology, Behaviour and Social Networking*, 2014

[3] Cacioppo, John T., Cacioppo, Stephanie, Gonzaga, Gian C., Ogburn, Elizabeth L., et. al., 'Marital Satisfaction and Break-Ups Differ Across Online and Offline Meeting Venues', *Proceedings of the National Academy of Sciences of the United States of America*, 2013

were very nice, but I just wasn't giving anyone enough time. I always thought there was someone better out there.'

This hope for someone better has made some of us eternally dissatisfied with the whole dating experience. Researchers call this a 'rejection mindset' which is a result of choice overload.[4] We are more likely to reject perfectly eligible matches when we have too many choices. So perhaps the best way to navigate this landscape of unlimited choices is to try out one potential partner at a time. Not only might this prevent choice paralysis, it might also prevent unnecessary hurt.

[4] Pronk, Tila M., Denissen, Jaap J. A., 'A Rejection Mindset: Choice Overload In Online Dating', *Social Psychology And Personality Science*, 2019

Exes, Boys' Nights, Lovers and Lies

'Everyone has skeletons in their closet.'

— Tushar, thirty-six

'You know, Prach, ask any woman I've ever slept with what she thinks of me and I guarantee you not one will have anything bad to say,' twenty-four-year-old Karan tells me. Karan is tall and muscular and gives you all his attention when he talks to you. Never mind that the undivided attention may only last until he spots an attractive woman. Notorious among his friends for 'having it easy with the girls', I can see how young women are charmed by him. He's someone who likes to 'breadcrumb'. At the same time, Karan doesn't try to conceal the fact that he is interested only in sex, sometimes preceded by drinks and dinner, sometimes not. He doesn't mislead the women he seduces into believing that there's more on the table. He keeps it simple and knows what he wants. 'Now if a woman gets attached to me, that's not my fault,' he tells me. And then, 'I mean I don't blame them,' he winks. 'But I know what I want. If I am ever in a relationship, it will be exclusive and committed. I'm clear about that. Unless I meet someone who I think I can be with, I don't like to get emotionally involved.'

In Delhi cliques, everyone is separated only by three degrees. As it were, I met one of Karan's casual hook ups at a party. Confident and outspoken, with a great sense of humour and an enviable job at a fashion magazine, this twenty-six-year-old had a distant look and smiled to herself when Karan came up in conversation. 'Yeah, he was fun,' she tells me. 'But he's not someone I'd ever be with. Not my type.'

Compare this with Arjun, a twenty-seven-year-old who likes to sweet talk his FWB, to tell them they are special and that he thinks the world of them — each one of them. Arjun has earned a bad rap because he's led some of his FWBs to believe they were the only ones he was hooking up with at the time. But stuff like this spreads like wildfire.

'You always know when something is up. I asked him so many times if there was someone else, if there was something he wanted to tell me. I gave him so many chances, but he never fessed up,' Shreya, one of Arjun's many jilted FWBs tells me. 'If he had been honest with me, I'd have let it go. You can't keep telling me I'm the only one and then say that to ten other women. I mean if you don't want exclusivity, you can say it. We're all grown ups here.' When Shreya found out he was saying the same thing to the other women he had slept with she could no longer believe that it was 'just for the sex'.

Another young woman tells me of an erstwhile lover who, in her words, 'Cheated on someone else, but cheated me.' Nishtha's story highlights an interesting aspect of dishonesty — that men and women don't lie, they just don't tell. 'I knew all along that he wasn't ready for commitment or exclusivity. Though it bugged me a little. I was okay with it because the truth is I wasn't looking for anything serious either. So I was okay with his non-committal approach to whatever it was that we were doing, knowing very well that he was sleeping around with other women. Until one day, I discovered that he had a girlfriend. And I mean, a steady relationship of five years — not someone he had recently met or was on the fence about. Man, I was livid! In that moment, I realized that he wasn't playing fuckboy because he didn't want commitment. He was basically a lying, cheating asshole who made me his whore without my knowledge. *That's* why I felt cheated — because he made me the other woman and I didn't even know it.'

Attraction is not always linear, and feelings of love fluctuate too. As if the innate vicissitudes of a relationship weren't enough, matters are further complicated by blurred boundaries, complex social circles and a life motto based on 'following one's heart's desires' (because, you know, YOLO or you only live once). This leads to a mesh of all sorts of lovers and loves — the one who got away, the one who is in your arms, the one you'll never have, the one you almost had, the one you want only for the night, the one you want for life — and often leads to situations that end up leaving undeserved scars in their wake. Dishonesty and betrayal are no longer as simple as having an affair and hiding the fact from your partner. Relationships now are often vague and ambiguous, and this unclear definition opens room for interpretation. What one may consider a breach, the other may not. There is a lot of not knowing — not knowing how to define certain alliances, not knowing what the appropriate behaviour is when dealing with an ex, a crush, a one-night stand, where the boundaries lie with a good friend with whom there may be a spark, and finally, with your partner — not knowing how much sharing is warranted or expected.

Yes, relationships today are plagued by dishonesty but is all dishonesty deceit?

MEN DON'T LIE. THEY JUST DON'T TELL THE TRUTH.

While talking to men about honesty and lies in relationships, I was reminded of a crucial lesson about communication and humans: the words we use matter. In fact, they are a game-changer.

When I first started asking the question 'What do you lie about to your partner?', eight out of ten men responded saying they don't lie. Some made sure to tell me about their personal philosophy that brutal honesty was the cornerstone of a strong and healthy relationship.

I didn't believe it. I couldn't believe that so many men out there were being 100-percent honest with their partner. Surely, they must tell some white lies, if not lies about another woman? I reframed the question and asked the same men: 'What do you do when something is important to you but your partner doesn't approve of it?'

People lie for various reasons — to get attention, to get something they want and to avoid conflict. According to Chandra, in relationships, the most common reason why people lie is to avoid conflict. By rephrasing my question, I had tapped into the common conflicts men face between their personal desires and pleasing their partner. Here's what they told me:

'Sometimes I go for drinks with the boys after work and I don't tell my girlfriend.'

'I don't tell my girlfriend everything about my family. I don't want her to have any preconceived notions. But if the relationship gets serious, and we decide to get married, then I'll tell her.'

'I'm still in touch with my ex but my girlfriend doesn't know.'

'If I want to go out clubbing or something, I don't always tell my partner. It just leads to unnecessary arguments. I don't want that headache.'

A few told me they hold back their honest opinions about things like their girlfriend's sartorial choices and friends because they don't want to hurt their feelings.

Tushar and I first began talking when I posted this question on social media. 'Everyone has skeletons in their closet,' he replied. We exchanged a few text messages before we got on a video call.

Tushar has the candour of a self-assured and well-satisfied individual. He doesn't fumble or hesitate and seems to have thought long and hard about his answers. Tushar is happily married to his long-term girlfriend. A few months ago, the couple had a beautiful baby girl. He later sends me pictures, so I can vouch for this.

But Tushar also has a lover. He met Mitali through a mutual friend, a year after he met his wife. Tushar had just moved to Mumbai. 'I was starting this new life in Mumbai. It was the first time I was living away from home and in a big city. I wanted to explore,' he tells me.

Mitali and Tushar started meeting for coffee, drinks, movies and dinners, and within a few weeks, they were hooking up. 'With Mitali, it was always casual. It was never love. But initially, I didn't tell her I had a girlfriend.'

That initial phase of Tushar inventing clever tactics to keep the two women a secret from each other lasted for eight months. Since he couldn't set rules for his girlfriends, Tushar had to set some rules for himself. When he was with Mitali, his phone would be on airplane mode so his girlfriend couldn't reach him. As much as possible, he would try to meet Mitali after he had had his nightly call with his girlfriend. On Sundays, Tushar would tell his now-wife that he was out playing cricket with his colleagues while he'd be playing hooky with Mitali.

Needless to say, all that dodge-balling became exhausting for Tushar and he decided to spill the beans to Mitali. 'She was very chill about it. She didn't mind that I had a girlfriend.' That, he tells me, changed everything. Now there was only one woman he was lying to, and that was easy to manage.

DISHONESTY IS CULTURAL

Infidelity is as commonplace as marriage is a premium in our country. Call it our culture's hypocrisy, or the current generation's crisis, but as I'm told, and as I observe first-hand, a remarkably large number of married people — men, and women — in urban India are committing some form of adultery. In a survey of 1,525 married Indians, 55 per cent admitted to cheating on their spouse.[5]

[5] Staff, 'Married Women In India Are Finding Love Outside Their Marriages. Is This Bad News?', *News18*, 6 March, 2021

Like Tushar, many don't feel guilty about it. It fulfils a need, and they are okay living a double life. Or, as Chandra puts it, a life of *jugaad. Jugaad* is a uniquely Indian concept. Defined as a 'uniquely flexible approach to problem-solving that uses limited resources in an innovative way,' this makeshift approach has led to many clever inventions. But in relationships, this attitude is only a temporary fix, or more accurately, a false sense of problem-solving.

To solve relationship problems, we need several resources — openness to learning and growth, patience and understanding, and most importantly, communication. In most Indian families, communication is abysmal. We seldom challenge familial structures and hierarchy, and this leads to a culture of either compliance or silent rebellion.

After Prince Harry and Meghan Markle appeared on *Oprah* to talk about their exit from the royal family, there was much furore on social media about how they had maligned the royal family. One Twitter account whose tweets are often representative of how men think, posted: 'So Harry the husband told his wife while she was pregnant, this horrible & painful thing that her kid's skin color was a matter of concern in his family. Isn't this an absolute scumbag behavior. Husbands are supposed to be lightning rods, to diffuse tensions between the two sides.'[6] In other words, lie to your wife to avoid stirring the family pot. Protecting the wife, in this case, sounds like a poor excuse cloaked in benevolent sexism.

---

[6] https://twitter.com/GabbbarSingh/status/1369133010977624069

This approach, though, is not uncommon, and this too, like many other harmful behaviours, begins in childhood. Many of us who are now in our late twenties and thirties were raised by parents who didn't encourage dialogue. We were given instructions, fables and moral lessons that were taught as absolutes. When a child asked 'why?' Most parents would hush the child up by saying something to the effect of 'because I said so' or 'because *aise hi hota hai* (it is what it is)'. Chandra also reminds me that when parents set different rules for their children without explaining why, while doing the same things they forbid their kids, children learn to mirror that hypocritical behaviour. 'Lying begins in childhood. When parents don't encourage kids to question and show hypocritical behaviour. A simple example is when parents drinking alcohol themselves in front of the kids don't let the child drink without explaining why.' If we want to change this culture of lying and hiding, young parents must learn to have open and honest conversations with their kids and avoid hyperboles like '*aise hi hota hai*'.

For the generation that raised us, opposite sex relationships were linear and clearly defined. You largely stayed away from the other sex until someone caught your fancy. Then, you pursued them. Regardless of sexual involvement, if you spent time with a member of the opposite sex one-on-one and there was flirtatiousness in the air, you were considered to be exclusively romantically involved. Dating existed in its own form but with the pointed aim of marriage. This meant that you dated someone you saw yourself marrying one day and then you married them.

Now, however, we date for many reasons — for sex, to pass time, to explore and to date for the sake of dating. For an increasing number of people, marriage is no longer the end goal of dating. Yet, often, we may date someone we really like, or even love, but end up marrying someone else. Our society is caught between two cultures — one that still upholds traditional values, considers marriage a family business, with little or no regard for the groom or bride's desires, and another that considers marriage a union between two people, with families coming together only as a byproduct. Now, some people break away from this dilemma and either fully submit to the arranged marriage route or commit to finding a life partner of their liking. But many end up in relationships with someone of their choosing and marriage with someone of their family's. This leads to many broken hearts and a culture of dishonesty that is too systemic to be blamed entirely on one individual.

Many couples end up in Chandra's clinic to seek help dealing with infidelity. This 'double life' reminds me of the silent rebellion many of us had as teenagers — telling our parents we are out at tuition while we go on a date, wearing a kurta over a noodle strap top which is then removed the minute we're out of our parents' sight, going on trips with a boyfriend/girlfriend while using one's best friend as alibi, pretending one has never tasted alcohol when just the previous weekend one was at a house party with contraband, so on and so forth.

For most of us, this was a way of life as teenagers. But some of us seem to have gotten arrested at this stage. We still do the same things, except, with our partners instead of our parents. As children and adolescents, we hid things from our parents because we feared punishment. As adults, we often hide things from our partner because of the same fear.

Sometimes, we lie to our partners because we want to maintain an illusion of perfection. Tushar tells me that his wife thinks he is the 'perfect husband'. When he is with her, he brings his best to the table, and this serves them well. More specifically, it serves him well. 'I don't want her to think I failed to be a good husband.'

DOES HONESTY EXIST IN A VACUUM?

'My wife is too trusting. She believes anything I tell her. When we were dating and I'd tell her I'm going out with friends, she would never ask who, which friends. She would believe me,' Tushar tells me. I ask him what she should've done differently. 'If she would have asked me for more information, questioned me, I probably would have not got too involved with Mitali. Because I wouldn't want to cause fights with my wife.' He then tells me women shouldn't be this gullible, that if we don't keep a tight leash on the men we date or we'd end up with someone like him. Yet, no guilt for having an affair. One can't make generalizations based on individual stories but we know that men get away with many things because we, as a society, don't hold them accountable. Honesty, communication, accountability — they are all interconnected. If we don't encourage open dialogue, we can't possibly create an ethos of honesty. If we don't create an ethos of honesty, we can't hold each other accountable and don't learn to hold ourselves accountable.

Unfortunately, in relationships, it often falls upon women to cultivate communication, honesty and accountability. Jacob, a techie living in Bengaluru, learnt about the importance of honesty in relationships only after he and his girlfriend had had a fair number of fights about his behaviour. To bond with his new colleagues at his first job, he would often accompany them to a hookah bar after work. His girlfriend did not like it. She didn't have a problem with him hanging out with his colleagues post work, but she detested the idea of her boyfriend sitting in the corner of a dingy hookah bar, sucking on a pipe passed among a group of potbellied men. Jacob, however, felt obliged to tag along with his colleagues. To get away with this, he began lying to his girlfriend. When he started taking her along to office parties — Diwali, birthdays, etc. — someone or the other would start reminiscing about the good old hookah bar, unknowingly spilling Jacob's long-held secrets. This happened a few times, and when his girlfriend finally told him she would leave him if he didn't stop, he stopped. Lying. He stopped lying. Not going to the hookah bar with his colleagues.

'I still go, once in ten days or so but now I tell my girlfriend. I know she doesn't like it. She gets upset a little. But all that lying is not worth it. It's too much trouble,' he tells me.

According to Chandra, 'psychological nakedness' — the ability to be emotionally and psychologically authentic and vulnerable with another person is crucial in healthy relationships. Without this, he says, one can't have true intimacy.

But sometimes psychological nakedness is met with critique and judgement. Ken Solin, author of *Act Like a Man*, a book about eight men examining and unlearning dysfunctional patterns as fathers, partners and friends, and learning new ways of relating, writes, 'The way a woman responds to a man's emotional honesty determines whether or not he'll feel safe enough to be emotionally honest again.'[7]

This isn't about gender though. It's human nature and it is equally true when the tables are turned. This means that how a man responds to a woman's emotional honesty also determines if she'll feel safe enough to be emotionally honest again. This is a common sight in many Indian households. Women hide their struggles and complaints from men because they fear that their husband, brother or father will get angry. This kind of dishonesty which stems from fear of how the men will react goes beyond the family and can manifest in any kind of dynamic — between an employee and employer, a parent and child, siblings and even friends. Sometimes, this anticipation of unpleasantness prevents men from being honest with their partner.

When I called Pradyum the day before the 2021 lockdown began, my intention was to set up a time for a video call. He and I had been chatting for a while and we had had some insightful conversations about male sexuality, digital media, books and music. I wanted to deep dive into his love life to which he generously agreed. What was supposed to be a quick ten-minute call lasted an hour and a half. With a sense of urgency,

[7] Solin, Ken, 'Men Who Fear Emotional Honesty', *Huffington Post*, 30 April, 2012

he tells me about his marriage, his ex-girlfriend, his best friend, work and kids. He always knew he was going to have an arranged marriage. He still thought about his ex-girlfriend sometimes and has forgiven his best friend who 'stole' her from him. He enjoys his work and loves his kids. He thinks his wife — whom he loves very much — feels insecure because she's not as educated as him or some of his friends.

An hour and a half later, he is home. He has to park his car and go in, but he regrets cutting the call short. I have questions. I ask if we can set up a Zoom call for later in the week. 'I'd love to say hi to your wife and kids too!' I tell him. 'Yeah, I don't think my wife and kids will be able to meet you. Let's do the Zoom call when the lockdown is over. My wife will get worried about who this Prachi is and I don't want her to know I'm talking to you. She'll worry unnecessarily,' he tells me.

Chandra tells me that many young men don't tell their partner if they are talking to another woman even when they are just friends. They worry about worrying their partner. How ill-equipped are we at showing our love and reassuring our loved ones!

WHAT HAPPENS WHEN MEN ARE LIED TO?

Sanchit is currently single and not interested in dating anyone. At thirty-one, he is of 'ripe age', as he says. He has had two girlfriends in the past — one while he was an engineering student in IIT Roorkee, and the other when he was a working man in Silicon Valley. 'Both of them cheated on me and both cheated with my friends,' he tells me. 'The first one cheated with my batchmate with whom I had a study group. The second one cheated on my roommate. And it happened to me in both countries, so it's not like an Indian or an American thing. It was terrible because not only had my girlfriends lied, my friends had also lied to me. I have shut down. I keep people at bay now because if my own friends could do that, then anyone can.'

When Rachit's ex-girlfriend cheated on him, he couldn't believe it. I ask him if he couldn't believe she had done it or that it had happened to him. 'That it had happened to me,' he tells me. When it sunk in, he was angry at her, until he 'got over it' and moved on.

While the most common lies in relationships have to do with infidelity, this isn't the only form of betrayal. Vidur had a girlfriend back in Ludhiana. He first met her at a chai stall at a college fest. They exchanged glances and made small talk about the delicious chai. He ran into her a few times through the day. The fourth time he spotted her, he gathered the courage to strike a longer conversation with her. They started dating soon after. She was in her final year of MBBS at Christian Medical College. She had two sisters and she was the middle child. Her father hated dogs while her mother fed the dogs in the street. A few months after they started dating, Vidur moved to Gurugram for work. They continued seeing each other once a month, either in Ludhiana or Gurugram. When it was time for his girlfriend to graduate with a medicine degree, Vidur started insisting she look for opportunities in Delhi; she could work for a year or two before studying further. 'That's when I found out she had lied. She was not doing her MBBS — she had dropped out of college after her first year.' The two broke up. 'Integrity is very important for me,' says Vidur. But it took a long time for him to heal and move on from that betrayal. 'I was so depressed. I felt so stupid for believing her.'

While lies may have a gender, betrayal stings just the same for everyone.

Are Romance and Chivalry Dead?

> *'When I open a door for a woman — and I do if she's sitting in the passenger seat of my car — it varies. Sometimes women are like WTF. Sometimes they appreciate it. But it* [opening the door] *makes me feel good. It's the same as making a cup of coffee for someone I like. Or a meal. Or playing a song... I like making them happy.'*
>
> — Venkat, thirty-six

In a culture where splitting the bill and taking Ubers to date night is becoming the norm, what happens to the script of romance? Historically, romance has been skewed towards expecting the man to carry the baton of wooing while the woman follows his lead. The man pursues and the woman relents. But as women become more independent — financially, emotionally, sexually — sweet nothings and pick-me-ups are fast losing their worth. Top that with quick swipe lefts, quicker swipe rights and even quicker half-goodbyes. You get the drift...we are either too independent, too 'cool', too frivolous or simply too busy to think about romance. We are too 'woke' to indulge in gestures that seem superficial and allegedly lack the depth of real love and connection. But is romance superficial and unnecessary to love?

In her book, *Ambition and Accommodation*, author Roberta S. Sigel talks about how many people view gender equality and romance as incompatible.[8] As women become independent and craft successful careers for themselves, becoming self-sustaining and achieving higher status in society, the need to attract a high-status mate diminishes. If a woman makes her own money, goes around in powerful circles, can take herself on an international trip, can protect herself, she doesn't need a man to chaperone her through everyday life. She makes her own place in society. This — a woman coming into her own and becoming her own messiah — is deemed antithetical to romance. But we often forget that the need for a man or a companion runs deeper than its functional benefits. That to partner up is an innate human need, which doesn't diminish by becoming self-reliant. What does change is *how* we partner up.

Experts say that romance is important, and its value supersedes the initial wooing stages of a relationship. Contrary to what we may believe, romance becomes more significant as a relationship grows.[9] Sure enough we have multiple industries that have monetized the chase of romance — classics like *Romeo and Juliet* that have stood the test of time; movies that give us silent goosebumps and embarrassing tears and melt our stubborn hearts; lyrics that could put any cynic

[8] Roberta Sigel, 'Ambition and Accommodation', *University of Chicago Press*, 1996

[9] 'The Importance of Romance in a Relationship in the United States in 2019', Statistica Research Department, 12 December 2019

to shame; days like Valentine's Day that celebrate love and the gift shops that stock up on V-Day specials; jewellery businesses that keep making engagement rings bigger and pricier; and of course, hashtag relationship goals that has many singles and couples across the globe itching for that special feeling. The wedding industry, with its trimmings of customized everything, is an emblem of modern-day romance. In modern relationships, romance seems to have become less personal and more pompous.

WHY ROMANCE?

We want to be made to feel special and we want to make the person we love feel special. We want them to know that they are unlike any other. This is where romantic gestures step in, and perhaps this is what makes romance an issue we all ponder over, regardless of which side of the debate we favour. Despite its popularity, not many people appreciate the effort that goes into romantic gestures. One can't deny that much thought and work goes into planning the perfect anniversary dinner or proposal. More so, in maintaining a romantic spark through a long-term relationship — remembering to bring flowers on birthdays, being thoughtful enough to leave love notes or kissing goodbye before heading to work or making sure you still seduce each other even after all these years of being together. Romance is work. But why exactly do we need to do this work? Isn't simply being there for someone enough?

Turns out, it's not. I asked a hundred people between the ages eighteen and thirty-five about the relevance of romance in a relationship, and four patterns emerged from their responses[1]:

1. TO DEMONSTRATE FEELINGS, LOVE, INTEREST AND DESIRE

Unsurprisingly, this was the most popular thought behind why we indulge in romantic gestures — to convey their feelings and interest. Note that this has little to do with the person at the receiving end, but rather a way of expressing one's desires to a love interest. No wonder initiating romance has been the prerogative of men. Men have been the ones to ask a woman out on a date, make the first move, and when ready for marriage, propose.

Bumble has turned this around. On this revolutionary app, only women can start a conversation after a match. It has taken agency away from men and given it to women. Men seem to have mixed views about this. Aadil finds it annoying. 'Sometimes you really want to talk to someone you match with and they don't text you. It just makes you feel so helpless.' Aayan finds the idea interesting but doesn't like to wait to start a conversation. He had one serious relationship in the past and was casually dating at the time of this conversation. Bumble is a lesson in patience for men.

Outside the world of women-powered dating apps, several young women are taking on the baton of romancing and wooing a man, and some men are loving this. 'I think it's really cool when a girl asks a guy out and tells him what she wants. It takes the pressure off men. I've dated two girls who asked me

[1] Survey.

out and it was just different. I didn't have to keep second-guessing whether they are really into me or not,' Aayan tells me.

2. TO IMPRESS

Planning a day full of feel-good whispers, topped with gourmet meals (perhaps with heart-shaped cookies?), a goosebump-inducing playlist at a heart-melting venue is certainly a show of one's thoughtfulness and pampering skills. A way to say, 'Hey! Look at me. Look at what I can do for you! Look at what *I* can do.' A display; a performance, if I may say so? Like a peacock spreads its feathers in a breathtaking show of beauty and virility, the man puts on a show of his ability to shower attention, flattery and be present in the form of a grand romantic gesture. Women also have their own ways of impressing a potential partner. Romance, then, may as well be a mating call.

3. TO RISE ABOVE THE MUNDANE

Romantic gestures usually require thorough planning and aren't something we do on a daily basis. A surprise birthday party, a vacation for two, a fancy dinner, don't usually figure in one's daily to-do list. Life can be mundane and boring. As is a relationship, even a healthy one. Romance can offer a way out of the mundane. One tip offered by psychologists and relationship coaches to long-term couples is that they must continue going on date nights. To keep a relationship from becoming stale, it is important to keep *dating* each other — to dress up and look good for each other, buy each other gifts for no reason, to discover new places and new things together, to keep the wonder alive!

For Jaiwin and his long-distance girlfriend, small gestures go a long way in breaking the monotony of video calls. Every now and then, they surprise each other with an impromptu visit or send an unexpected present. For Jaiwin, this is easy to do. He is a budding athlete who moved to Delhi from Jaipur to train. His girlfriend still lives in Jaipur. The distance isn't much, and he can hop on a bus on a Friday evening and be back in Delhi on a Sunday night for an early morning training session on Monday.

4. TO CREATE MEMORIES

This is where romance begins to become a shared pursuit of intimacy and joy rather than a rehearsed tactic employed to win someone's approval. At some point in the relationship, the wooing stops and both partners are expected to nurture the relationship. Romance, at this stage, becomes a tool to create new memories and build a treasure trove of nostalgia that can outlive even their love for each other. For couples in long-term relationships, it's the little things that only they share that keep the romance alive.

Pradyum and his wife like going for long drives to find a spot where they can share a few beers in the car. He brings this up a few times in our conversation, and it seems to me this shared ritual is important to him.

Jacob and his girlfriend take frequent road trips. It's their time away from work and friends, and they especially enjoy the long drives where they aren't distracted by their phones. 'We can talk for the entire four to five hours of driving. The drive is the best part of our road trips.'

WHAT ROMANCE IS NOT

Alain de Botton, a contemporary British philosopher, talks in depth about how the Romantic period has influenced our present day understanding of romance and how it may be inadvertently sabotaging our chances at finding and keeping true love.[2] The eighteenth-century Romantics believed life must be lived with intense emotionality, a heavy dose of individualism and a generous sprinkling of idealism. They believed that for an experience to be valuable, it must have the power to move us, satiate our desires and embody perfection.

Now, apply this philosophy to love and what do you get?

Intense emotionality = Having an all-or-nothing approach to love, that you're either madly, blindly, wholly in love with each other or nothing at all.

Individualism = Believing that love is enough to make a relationship last. That love is an individual entity, complete and sustainable on its own.

Idealism = That a relationship and a partner must be perfect. So many myths about relationships are borne out of this idealistic approach, but I'll point out only the most common and damaging two. First, that we believe there are no fights or disagreements in healthy relationships, and second, that we expect our partners to be mind-readers, to somehow magically intuit what we want and what will make us happy.

---

[2] Button, Alain De, '*How Romanticism Ruined Love*', The School Of Life

Chandra cautions against all this. He insists that a black-and-white approach to relationships is impractical and sets us up for heartbreak and disappointment. 'We have to be okay with that grey area,' he says often.

Romance is not a magic pill that can ensure a happy relationship or winning over someone's heart. Like everything else in a relationship, romance needs to be backed up with other ways of making one's partner feel special. Nor is it a remedial balm when one does something hurtful. A friend tells me of an ex-boyfriend whose idea of romance was straight out of a Mills and Boons novel. It was the stuff of the dreams to be honest. One Valentine's Day that they spent apart, he arranged for a bouquet of flowers to be delivered to her house every hour from midnight to midnight. Twenty-four hours of the day of love, twenty-four bouquets of roses and lilies to fill his absence. That should have made her commit to a lifetime with him, right? Well, it did. Until a few months later, he confessed that he had spent the day with his ex-girlfriend and 'stuff happened'.

This brings me to another unique dilemma of modern relationships. These days, it's not uncommon for young people to date multiple people simultaneously. One can't assume exclusivity. In fact, unless it is explicitly discussed it may be safe to assume that the person you're chatting with on a dating app is also chatting with someone else. But where does that leave romance? If the purpose of romantic gestures is to make someone feel special, then must it not be exclusive? If your idea of romance is to bring flowers for your date, then is it still romantic if you're bringing flowers for all the three people you're currently dating?

I turn to Karan and Aadil — young, charming men who are dating multiple women. I want to understand the rules, if any, of early-stage romance when one is with more than one person. They have opposite views on romance, which makes me think there's another factor at play — one's personality.

Karan: 'It all depends. If the girl likes flowers and things like that I'll get her those. If there's something else she's into, I'll do that for her. Like once I dated this dog lover. She would feed the stray dogs in her colony and get jackets and blankets for them in winter. So I got kennels for her strays. It's not like I will do the same romantic thing for every girl. But yes, I will do what I can to make them feel special — isn't that the point of dating?'

Aadil: 'I'm not a romantic guy, man!' He then thinks about it for a moment. 'I used to make these playlists for my ex. I think that was romantic. But I'll do something like that only if I'm really into someone. Otherwise, it just feels like wasted effort.'

A FINE ROMANCE

There are many things that can be called romantic, but the ones that truly stick and matter in the long run are the small, unquantifiable ones — your inside jokes or the way you glance at each other to check-in at a party; remembering to keep the dishes in the sink and the toilet lid down; remembering important dates and making sure you celebrate them; learning their order at their favourite restaurant; putting one less spoon of sugar in the blender when you make cold coffee because that's how they like it; offering them a foot massage without them having to ask for it if they have had a long day. Love is in the details. Always.

Alain de Botton speaks of romantic realism as a way to ensure a satisfactory long-term relationship.[3] He suggests that we must shun the idea of perfection, that our partner must serve all our needs and that a relationship must always make us happy all the time. Making a commitment without any hope of perfection (with an approach of pragmatism rather than romanticism) means that one consciously and deliberately nurtures the relationship. That through actions, big and small, one develops deeper intimacy and commitment, and a life together that is based on sharing rather than flattery. This translates into dealing with everyday responsibilities as a team rather than two individuals, together rather than against each other. An egalitarian romance, then, means one person doing the cleaning while the other cooks; one person spending money on daily needs, while the other pays the down payment; one person dropping off the dry cleaning, while the other picks it up. It translates into stepping up to do things that will make your partner's life better on a daily basis.

When the basics are taken care of, it frees one emotionally to experience deeper human experiences. Psychologist Abraham Maslow theorized that our needs follow a hierarchy. He drew a pyramid to explain that in order to fulfil our higher selves — what he

---

[3] Botton, Alain De, '*Romantic Realism*', The School Of Life

calls self-actualization — we must first have our basic needs met and work our way up the pyramid.[4] At the base of this pyramid are physiological needs (food, water, shelter, clothing, etc.). Second comes safety (health, employment, family, etc.). Third comes love and belonging (friendship, family, intimacy, sense of connection). Number four is self-esteem (confidence, self-respect, accomplishment). On the top of the pyramid is self-actualization where we come into our authentic moral, emotional, selves with acceptance and a state of psychological flow. According to Maslow, we must climb these steps one at a time. We can't attain self-actualization unless we have everything else in place first. If you apply this logic to relationships, then this would mean that we can't feel intimate with someone unless our physiological and safety needs are first met. Apply this to the particular case of romance, and this would mean that occasional grand gestures are meaningless if on a daily basis; you don't make your partner feel heard and secure in the relationship!

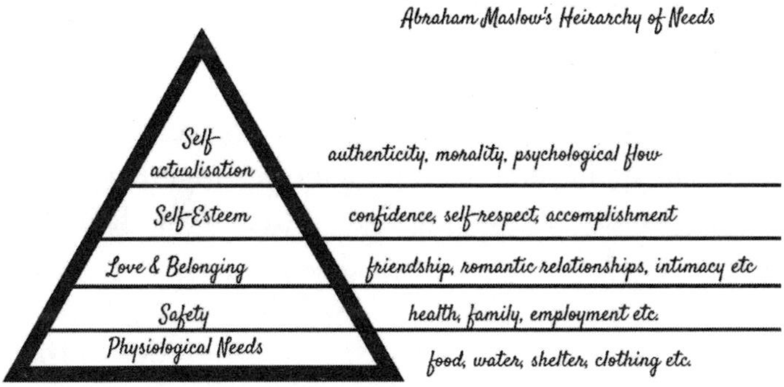

[4] Kaur, Avneet, 'Maslow's Need Hierarchy Theory: Applications And Criticisms', *Global Journal Of Management And Business Studies*, 2013

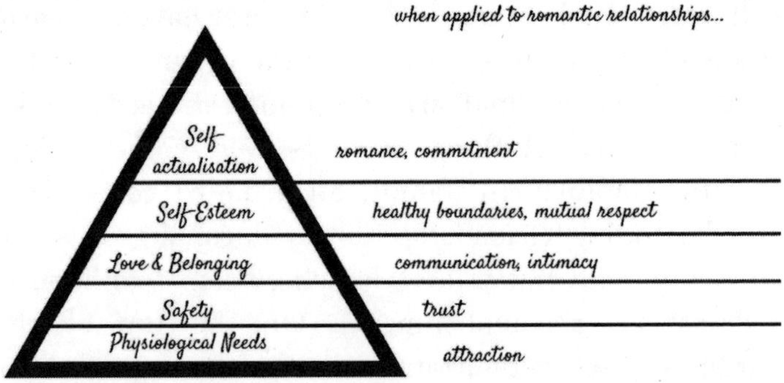

To put this in perspective, let's take the example of a cohabiting couple whose relationship is based on rigid gender roles. Traditionally, one person is burdened with the responsibility of taking care of the household while the other goes out into the world to earn their bread and butter. In this scenario, the couple spends most of their waking time apart, in remarkably different physical and mental spaces. When they reunite at the end of the day both are rightly exhausted. Romance in such a living arrangement demands an annual vacation and the occasional dinner date. Cherished as these may be, these moments are too few and far between, and too far removed from their everyday interaction and lives together. They may do a great job at rising above the mundane and even creating memories together. But do these grand gestures improve intimacy in their daily lives?

Now, take the example of a cohabiting couple whose relationship is based on shared responsibilities. Perhaps they take turns to cook or decide the menu for the night so their home chef can stir it up! Buying groceries and decor for the house is not the woman's job alone, and the man also has a say in the colour of curtains for their living room. He contributes with more than just money. Maybe they both have jobs, and even if one makes less, the onus of financial security doesn't fall on only one person's shoulders. There is a sense of teamwork rather than tasks delegated to individuals in a big venture. In this context, romance may mean one person making sure the kitchen is clean for the other to cook. Or one taking the other out for a fancy dinner to uplift their mood when the other is stressed. Intimacy comes in stolen kisses while cooking dinner together. It's in the details. The annual vacation may still be there, but a more equal and intimate dynamic in your relationship opens up possibilities of different kinds of romance. Who wouldn't want that?

Twenty-three-year-old Namita, who is in a committed relationship and who defines romance as 'bringing flowers, flirting with each other, being all mushy', believes that it's okay if romance is absent. 'After a while you become best friends,' she says. I ask what she means by that. She explains: 'I think that when two people like each other, they spend more time with each other than anybody else. They know more about each other than anyone else, hence they end up becoming best friends. The couple knows about each other's moods, likes and dislikes, etc., better than anyone else. They even end up judging people in a similar manner! Romance becomes less important as you spend more time together. In a new relationship, there is more excitement because you are slowly getting to know a person's romantic side. But, in my opinion, romance is not the thing that keeps the couple going. It fades over time. It's the mutual understanding that keeps love strong. And you go through life with your best friend. What could be better than that?'

The essence of friendship is caring, acceptance, a sense of protectiveness, playfulness and camaraderie. With these elements in the mix, the need for extravagant gestures diminishes, and is replaced by practical, hands-on supportive gestures that are necessary for smooth everyday functioning. Yes, things like not throwing wet towels on the bed and folding the laundry. But does that mean you don't have to do anything romantic ever for your best friend who doubles as your significant other once you are settled in your relationship? No, let's not kill romance. Let's understand that it comes in many forms, and the small, daily details of love matter as much as those special occasions.

A NOTE ON CHIVALRY

When I was dating, I had a simple rule that helped me screen men. On the first date, if a guy didn't make sure I reached home safely or asked me to text once I was home or checked on me to make sure I'd reached, he was not worth my time. As part of the goodbye, I expected a remark about this or a text message inquiring about my whereabouts within an hour of us departing. This is not because I couldn't make it home safe on my own. I could — and have been doing so for more than a decade. It is because I live in one of the most unsafe Indian cities for women and expect the man I'm with to be cognizant of this. Beyond this, I wouldn't expect a man to pick me up or drop me home or open the door for me or pull out the chair for me at a restaurant. I would, however, expect him to pick up that coffee jar from the top cupboard. Again, not because I can't do it myself — I will find a way — but because it's a simple act of kindness.

Some would brush off this kindness as chivalry — a set of actions that display men's greater physical strength and the meaning and intent of these actions has come to reflect the same — an imperious show of male strength. Over the years, chivalry has received some backlash because acts such as pulling out a chair for a woman or opening the door for her, tend to belittle us. So I decided to ask men their intentions behind chivalrous behaviour and the reactions they received.

Venkat Subramanyam, a thirty-something-year-old musician from Mumbai, tells me that he doesn't think too much about these acts of chivalry and habitually opens doors and pulls out chairs for women. 'When I open a door for a woman — and I do if she's sitting as a passenger in my car — it varies. Sometimes women are like WTF. Sometimes they appreciate it,' he tells me of their reactions. But he remains unfazed by the mixed bag. He goes on to say, 'It [opening the door] makes me feel good. It's the same as making a cup of coffee for someone I like. Or a meal. Or playing a song… I like making them happy.'

Dhairya tells me that in his experience, 'Chivarly is mocked.' I ask him to elucidate. He tells me his acts of kindness, or chivalry, aren't reserved for members of the opposite sex. 'So I'm usually the first one to let others walk in or out of the train, elevators, rooms, giving me way on a busy street. Once in office, I opened the door for a female colleague to let her pass before me. She acknowledged my gesture, but then I got mocked by some of the team members. "Dhairya always wants to look good," they said.' The same actions are interpreted differently in different contexts — when Dhairya opens the door for an elderly or male colleague, it's seen as an act of politeness, but when he does so with someone he could potentially date, it's seen as a tactic to make a good impression.

Some men, paralyzed in face of this social conundrum, don't display any act of kindness unless explicitly asked, and we, collectively complain that chivalry is dead. According to a survey conducted by the dating website Match, 73 per cent women agreed wholeheartedly that chivalry has become archaic.[1]

CHIVALRY OR CHAUVINISM?

Is chivalry dying because we can't separate it from chauvinism? When kindness is extended only as a bait for something in return, that's not chivalry; it's chauvinism. There's also a fine line between showing kindness and taking the reigns. It is crucial to understand the difference between the two. Rachit points out that some behaviours that may seem gentlemanly and intended to take the load off a woman may not always be so. 'If I'm out on a date with someone and I place the order on her behalf without asking her, that's not chivalry. I can maybe order for her once I've asked her what she'd like, and if she says she doesn't care, but not assume what she would want. Many guys do this though.'

Many men do this. It's pretty simple why this is inappropriate. In doing so, men rob the woman of a

[1] Reid, Rebecca, '73% Of Women Say That Chivalry Is Dead', *Metro*, 7 August, 2017

choice and the opportunity to make her own decision. This is chauvinism — a sense of superiority one feels towards the group they belong to.

Now, let's consider another common scenario. Many 'chivalrous' men diligently follow the routine prescribed as good behaviour — they open doors for women, offer to carry bags, give up their seats and pull out the chair. This is all very well and may seem kind and thoughtful, but when it comes to demonstrating kindness where it matters, they fail. They come home, kick off their shoes, put their feet on the table and expect to be served. They treat women they court or their partners with a sense of entitlement. They expect the woman to cook for them, keep the house clean and organized single-handedly while they accumulate trash, keep tabs on her whereabouts at all times and dictate who she speaks to, accept invitations on their behalf or otherwise assume that she will be available at his beck and call. There is no kindness in this. Chauvinism, then, emanates from a sense of entitlement too.

Many argue that chivalry is a dated concept. Indeed, it originated during medieval times. The term chivalry comes from the French word *chevalier*, which means 'horseman' or 'knight'.[2] Chivalry, back in the day, was the code of conduct expected of knights. A part of this was courteous behaviour towards those considered to be enemies and kindness and generosity towards those considered to be at a less advantageous position than oneself. A separate but related aspect of chivalry was

[2] Ashe, Laura, 'Love And Chivalry In The Middle Ages', British Library, 31 January, 2018

'courtly love', which referred to a singular dedication toward the pursuit of an unattainable woman. When courtly love and knightly chivalry are muddled together, we get the concept of knight in shining armour. It's this that women today don't want. She doesn't need a knight to come and rescue her from her 'disadvantageous position'. While we continue to associate chivalrous behaviour with this, it is important to note that by the fourteenth and fifteenth centuries, the term chivalry had evolved to refer to etiquette, and subsequently, contributed to what is considered gentlemanly behaviour today.

All this is very well but, unfortunately, in our male-dominated society, chivalry and chauvinism are deeply intertwined. Male chauvinism is often subtle and seeps into daily interactions, as is the case of the man who supports and maybe even celebrates his partner's professional success but doesn't do much to free her from domestic responsibilities. According to psychotherapists and authors Louis Bonino and Peter Szil, there's 'everyday chauvinism' at one end of the spectrum and 'death' (honour killing, partner death due to domestic violence, dowry deaths, etc.) at the other.[3] According to them, in between, in ascending order, are: ridicule, silencing, verbal violence, threats, pushing, slapping, kicking, breaking bones, burning and rape. All these are, ultimately, strategies for men to maintain power and control over women, which is what constitutes the definition of chauvinism.

[3] Bonino, Luis, Szil, Péter, Kuszing, Gábor, 'Everyday Male Chauvinism: Intimate Partner Violence Which Is Not Called Violence', *Daphne*, 2006

Chauvinism is a form of insidious violence that often goes unrecognized because many of these behaviours are passed down to us as 'normal' male behaviour and attitudes. The all-too-common dynamic mentioned before, where the man bears no responsibilities in the running of the household despite the professional and financial status of the woman is a classic example of what the authors call 'utilitarian everyday male chauvinism'. It is entrenched in the societal structure to train men to sit back and be served, while the woman runs around like a headless chicken to ensure that all his needs are met. Another common example is that of the man who feels entitled to sex.

Let's take a moment to note here how men and women have systematically been maintained as enemies, or opposites, or inherently too different to ever be able to understand each other and come at a level plane. The narrative of 'men are from Mars and women are from Venus' has kept us stuck in a tug of war for far too long. Domestic violence, sexual coercion and verbal abuse are now (finally) becoming unacceptable, but our work towards the two sexes finding a true union will not be over until we address the deep-rooted sense of male superiority — chauvinism — that is inherent in our society.

So how do we move past this uneven plane of coexistence that we maintain? How do we break the status quo?

The answer could lie in tapping into the human kindness that is innate in all of us, that surpasses sex and gender, age and religion, class and ethnicity. History may provide us with context but we are not slaves to it. History repeats itself only if we don't challenge it. Perceptions, functions and meanings evolve with culture. So to say that chivalry is a dated concept because its origins are tainted by inequality is defeatist. If we can rewrite history when it comes to architecture and technology, cultural practices and healthy living, then why can't we do it when it comes to how the sexes relate? Why must we be stuck in ways of the erstwhile? It sounds more like an excuse to not do the hard work of introspection and conscious living that is required to act from a place of kindness.

Allow me to paint you a picture. It may seem utopian, but hey, isn't the whole point of dialogues such as these to create a world that is utopian or an approximation of it? Let me introduce to you Sana and Sanjay. They have jobs that take up eight to ten hours of their day, they run a household with domestic help, possess furniture that is in pristine condition and a fridge that always has something to eat. They have a baby on the way, but they are not worried about drifting apart once they have the child. It may be a faint hum in the background somewhere because they are told this so often, but for now they are more concerned about having enough savings by the time the little one arrives. Their days together look somewhat likes this:

Sanjay wakes up before Sana does because he enjoys having the house to himself for the first hour or so. He heads to the kitchen and makes a pot of coffee, so that by the time Sana wakes up, there is a hot cup ready for her. The help comes shortly after and prepares breakfast while the duo get ready for work. They hop into their shared car, which Sana drives. She drops

Sanjay to work because his office is on the way. They come home around the same time, sometimes together, sometimes not. They split the rent and other bills. Sana is expecting a promotion and a considerable raise in her salary and they are looking for a bigger house because her increment will allow it. Cooking dinner is usually a shared chore — Sanjay chops, Sana stirs. Whoever finishes the meal last picks up the dishes. Usually, it's Sanjay. In the meantime, Sana gets dessert or tea ready. So their day goes. Neither is too burdened nor too nonchalant. It's their home, their life together and they nurture it just the same. Both are chivalrous to each other. Each will do what the other is less inclined or capable of.

Sanjay and Sana are a figment of my imagination. But these fictional characters are inspired by some real-life couples I've had the good fortune of knowing. They may not tick all the boxes, but they do tick enough for me to believe that this may be the future of marriage in urban India. Called 'peer marriage' by scholars, it is fast on the rise, and frankly, the need of the hour.[4] Characterized by shared income and shared responsibilities, this will put the fear that feminism is ruining family life, to rest. By attaining financial freedom, women have not only broken away from the shackles of patriarchal dependency, they have also become active contributors to prosperity of the couple. The same is required of men on the household front. Such partnerships require an even deeper level of understanding, patience and

[4] Arnold, Gaines, 'What Is A Peer Marriage? Definition And Characteristics', study.com, 2017

compromise compared to those based on traditional gender roles where responsibilities of daily upkeep don't intersect. And this, in turn, requires kindness — chivalry, if I may — by both sexes.

So, no, chivalry is not dead. In fact, it is needed now more than ever, though not in its knight-in- shining-armour avatar. Chivalry needs to be viewed from the lens of humanity and kindness, not gender. It needs to emanate from a place of pure nurturance.

PART FOUR

Marriage

The Courtship Period

'I really loved her but I broke up with her because my mother didn't think she would adjust in our family'
— Raul, twenty-nine

Aniket and Trisha tied the knot in early 2019. Theirs was a typical modern romance. They met on a dating app and were together for four years before Aniket proposed to her on a camping trip with friends. I met them at a party shortly after their wedding. With newlyweds in the room, inevitably, the conversation steered toward wedding preparations and celebrations. Another couple at the party were engaged and were in the thick of wedding preparations. The recent groom and the groom-to-be had much to bond over — how they finally decided it was time to get married, whether one should have a *baraat* or not, cocktail venues and honeymoon destinations.

At one point, Aniket began talking about how fights between Trisha and him escalated during the months preceding the wedding. Then he said something that defines the foundation of courtship and marriage in our country: 'For the boys' side, it's a celebration.

Girls' families are always more stressed out. Because you see…the boys' family is gaining a new member while the girls' family is losing one.' He meant to impart this hard-earned wisdom to his companion, to make him understand that he must be patient and understanding toward his fiancée and her family because they were giving up something for *him*. In the process, he ended up commodifying Trisha and all womankind and putting himself and all mankind on a pedestal.

This commodification is often accompanied by characterization. When marriage is on the table, so is the question: 'Is she good enough for me and my family?'

Raul is the youngest of three siblings, both sisters. One got married at nineteen and is a mom of two. The other is pursuing her PhD in the US. He met his ex-girlfriend in college. 'She was this cool girl in our engineering college. She played the drums, had short hair, used to chew gum in class,' he slaps his thigh and laughs, reminiscing about his 'wild ex'. 'I actually asked her to teach me how to play drums. That's how we started dating. Somehow…' he drifts off for a moment. 'I was nervous about introducing her to my family. I knew there would be some issue and I didn't want anybody to feel awkward.'

Raul devised a clever ploy to test the waters. On his visit back home during Diwali holidays, he decided to throw a party for his friends. He invited his school friends and some college friends who also came from Delhi. His ex-girlfriend, Stuti, was one of them. He told Stuti the parents wouldn't be around, so she needn't be nervous. Why? I asked him. 'She was a very strong-headed person and if I had told her she had to dress properly or not do something in front of my parents, she would have dumped my ass right there.'

At the time of the party, Raul's parents didn't know he had a girlfriend or that she was a guest. After the party, which according to Raul was 'good fun', he teasingly asked his mother what she thought about Stuti. '*Voh ladki jo beer pee rahi thi*? (That girl who was drinking beer?)'. Raul answered in the affirmative, but also pointed out that many people were drinking beer and other girls were drinking vodka too. His mother wasn't convinced. '*Nahi*,' she said. '*Badaa* low cut top *pehna tha usne* (She was wearing a low-cut top. I didn't like that).' Raul was nineteen at the time, which he explains was why he didn't know what was the right thing to do. 'I really loved her but I broke up with her [Stuti] because my mother didn't think she would adjust in our family.'

His relationship was put to a halt before he could even court the love of his life. Courting, or courtship, is different from dating. Courtship is entered into with the end goal of marriage. In arranged marriages, couples only court, they don't date. They enter the arrangement with one goal in mind: marriage. A couple introduced with the intent of matrimony either end up getting married or breaking up.

In India, when marriage comes up in conversation, so does the question: 'love or arranged'? When many young adults first start thinking about marriage, and if they haven't already found someone they want to marry, they are in this quandary.

Some people have a clear preference; they pick a side and stick to it. Some start off with the hope of marrying someone on their own terms but when they aren't able to find a long-term relationship in the dating pool, they settle for an arranged marriage, while others know from the beginning they will have an arranged marriage.

Even in a love marriage, a couple goes through a courtship period. Once their relationship is made official and the families know there is an impending wedding, something shifts. The girlfriend is now seen through the lens of the wife or daughter-in-law, and previously unspoken expectations are laid on the table. Some men tend to take a backseat at this point and let their family take the reins of welcoming their to-be daughter in law.

Courtship is said to be between the couple, but the ball is often in the family's court.

While the families scurry around to put together the perfect wedding and the to-be-bride dips her toes in the new role she's about to embark on, what are the men up to? I heard four types of stories. Some shocking and some pleasantly surprising. Let's start with the shocking — bad news first.

LAST INNINGS

Karthik had an arranged marriage. He always knew he would. He comes from a Brahmin family in a small town in south India. No one in his family has had a love marriage, and no one from the generations before his has moved to another city for education or work. 'When I was going to Manipal, my mother said, "You get a degree and a job and we will find a wife for you." So I knew.' He didn't meet his wife till after the marriage was fixed, and that too, only briefly and under his parent's supervision. These meetings were rare because he lived in another city. While his family prepared for the wedding, he was in Chennai meeting women on dating apps. 'Those were the last few months I'd be alone, and after my wife came to live with me, I wouldn't be able to do all that. So I went on many dates during my courtship period.'

Over the last few years, Vidur has attended several of his colleagues' weddings and been on several bachelors' trips. 'These bachelors' trips are always about hooking up,' he tells me. 'All these guys getting married are panicking. They think their life will be over and even if they're marrying their girlfriends, they want to have one last fling.'

This idea that a man's life is 'over' when he gets married is reinforced by other men. While women are told they are beginning a new life, going to a new home and are peppered with advice that will help them fulfil their new role, men's conversations often involve banter like, '*Ab toh tu phas gaya* (Now you're trapped).'

Aniket heard this from well-meaning uncles and older cousins who were married. But he, unlike Karthik and some of Vidur's colleagues, couldn't relate to the sentiment. He loved his to-be wife and couldn't see how marrying her was a 'trap'.

PASSING THE BUCK

The big fat Indian wedding places the bride in the spotlight, while the groom appears in the end to claim her. There are plenty of 'bridal packages' offered by salons, yoga teachers, dermatologists and nutritionists, but very few 'groom packages'. These services are geared toward preparing the bride-to-be to look her best on the wedding day. Of course, to look her best, the bride must also adorn the latest finery and jewellery. In fact, bridal couture is the only type of high fashion that works in India.[5] Wedding shopping begins for the bride and her family long before it does for the groom, and is far more extensive.

When Aniket asked his companion about the wedding preparations, he said, 'I don't have to do anything. Lekha [his fiancée] has a lot to do.' Their wedding is five months away, and Lekha is busy shopping for her trousseau. 'She's on this wedding app and is finding photographers and a DJ for the cocktail. She's managing most things. I just have to find a good outfit for the wedding day.'

'Yeah, even for us, Trisha was the one who did everything. All the decor and flower arrangements. I didn't have to do much.'

At this point, I interject and ask them if they would have liked to be more involved in the wedding preparations.

Aniket promptly responds, 'No, I'm okay. It's too much coordination. Let the families handle it.' His companion is torn. 'I want to plan all the fun stuff, but all these little things like flowers and the colour of the drapes and all, I don't care.'

SETTING BOUNDARIES

Toward the end of 2020, Jacob and his girlfriend decided to tie the knot. It was only after Jacob and his Bengali

[5] Vohra, Sanna, 'Significance Of Weddings For Indian Fashion Industry', Fibre2Fashion, March, 2020

girlfriend took the decision of getting married did they tell the families. Both families had inhibitions about cultural differences. He wanted his parents to speak to his girlfriend. Jacob's mother agreed, but his father refused to join the Zoom call. Only when the families were flown into Bengaluru for a meeting did his father acknowledge his girlfriend. The meeting went well, and the wedding was fixed for June 2021. Little did they know that another lockdown was on its way.

Jacob's parents were in Bengaluru for wedding preparations when the lockdown was announced. His girlfriend (he still doesn't call her his fiancée; it hasn't sunken in for him) lived alone in an apartment a few kilometres from his home, where his parents were now staying with him. They were working from home, and during the day Jacob would go over to her house. He'd spend the day with her — they'd work, cook and eat together. After dinner, he would come back to his parents' house to sleep. When the lockdown was announced, it no longer made sense for Jacob and his girlfriend to live in separate houses. With due permission from his parents, Jacob brought his to-be wife home.

'I think that was a big mistake,' he tells me. 'My parents are old fashioned, so it led to many misunderstandings in the beginning.'

'What kind of misunderstandings?' I ask.

'Like they would ask her to do things around the house. Small things like bringing them water, cleaning. But when my brother-in-law comes home, that's not expected of him. So, things like that.'

One day, Jacob explained to her mother that this differential treatment was not okay. Things have been better since then, he tells me. But his girlfriend is eagerly waiting for the lockdown to lift so she can move back to her apartment.

Some men take the courtship period as an opportunity to set boundaries between their future spouse and family. They become the spokesperson for the two sides, going back and forth, negotiating the terms of this new arrangement.

Nitin's wife did not want to live in the family home. She had grown up in a nuclear family and had been living on her own for a few years before they got married. She didn't want to give up her home and wanted Nitin to move in with him — the two of them to have a house of their own, and not live with Nitin and his family. Nitin comes from a joint family — parents, uncles and aunts and grandparents, all living under one roof.

For his family, watching their son move out instead of the daughter-in-law moving in was unpalatable. 'There was so much drama around that, I remember,' he tells me. 'I was okay either way. I think it would have been convenient living with my family. But if my wife is so uncomfortable with that idea, I would not want to put her through it. I have my family, and then I have a family with her now. I have to be more responsible to her. I want to make her happy.'

EMBRACING THE NEW LIFE

For most couples in India, the relationship is not taken seriously until the families approve. Most families in India approve only of marriage, not dating. So here's what happens: young people meet, fall in love, go through ups and downs and once they decide they want to commit to a lifetime with each other, they tell the families. When they get that stamp of approval from the family, it takes their relationship to the next level. The phase between deciding to get married and getting married brings with it a new level of intimacy for some people.

When Nitin entered the courtship period with his wife, he felt that he could now open up to her more easily. 'There are things you don't talk about unless you decide you are getting married — like your five-year plan, ten-year plan. After you get engaged, you start planning for two and not one.'

For many men, a big part of this planning is getting their finances in order, starting investments and savings for the future, and so on. For Nitin, the finances weren't a big concern because his wife earns well and brought her own savings and investments to the marriage. Even so, getting engaged prompted him to start thinking about when and where they would buy a house together, kids and retirement.

During this time, he also began trying to bond with her family and her sisters. 'She's very close to her sisters, and I know it's important to her that I have a good relationship with them. When we were dating, I would hang out with her and her sisters, but it was different. After getting engaged, I actually wanted to. I felt a new sense of responsibility toward her family that I didn't before.'

THE NEED FOR PREMARITAL COUNSELLING

Many to-be married couples don't have the necessary conversations Nitin and his wife had during their courtship period. Things like place of residence, kids, lifestyle, gender roles, work, work–life balance, finances are just brushed under the rug — sticky topics that can mar the celebratory mood.

Karthik and his wife interacted very little before they got married. This sometimes happens in arranged marriages where the families have more control than the bride and groom. In some cases, families meet and fix the marriage before the husband and wife are introduced to each other. In other cases, families shortlist a few prospectives and the bride or groom take their pick. In cases where the decision is left up to the prospective bride or groom after an introduction from matchmakers, they have more autonomy in decision-making. But communication is sometimes subpar.

Karthik agreed to marry his wife because 'his mother said so'. She liked her, and that was enough for Karthik. Away from home, from wedding preparations and his fiancée, Karthik had a 'duty-bound' marriage. He was marrying out of a sense of duty toward his parents, and he brought the motivation to his relationship with his wife. Could this have been prevented if communication between them was encouraged?

This lack of communication about future expectations is more common in arranged marriages, Chandra tells me. He offers premarital counselling to young couples. He tells me that most couples seeking premarital counselling are those who are about to get into an arranged marriage. Every now and then, Chandra meets couples who fight often and are in conflict-ridden relationships but they also want to get married. 'These couples with unresolved conflicts want clarity about their compatibility.'

When young couples seek premarital counselling, he assesses their personalities. He calls this a 'modern *kundli* matching' practice. Most importantly, he helps them have important conversations about their expectations. 'Marriage is complex. It's important to discuss your belief systems, your conflict resolution style, gender roles and plans. All this helps us figure out what kind of issues the couple may face in the future, and we can help them prepare for this.'

According to Chandra, in India, friends and relatives sometimes take on the responsibility of preparing the bride and groom for their life ahead. This is peppered with biases and stereotypes and does little to help create an egalitarian marriage. The growing popularity of premarital counselling in our country may be testament to the fact that young adults are breaking away from this orthodox mould of marriage.[6] More and more couples who meet through the traditional matchmaking route now want to create a marriage that is based on a solid foundation of open, honest communication. Those are the couples who end up in Chandra's clinic.

Premarital counselling can not only help improve the health of a relationship,[7] it can also make it more likely for the couple to seek help in the future.[8] Given

---

[6] Menon, Rajitha, 'Premarital Counseling Not So Rare Anymore', *Deccan Herald*, 9 October, 2019

[7] Parhizgar, Ozra, Esmaelzadeh, Sara, Kamrai, M.A., Rahimzadeh, Mitra, 'Effect Of Premarital Counseling In Marital Satisfaction', *Shiraz E. Medical Journal*, 2017

[8] Williamson, Hannah C., Hammett, Julia F., Ross, Jaclyn M., Karney, Benjamin R., Bradbury, Thomas N., 'Premarital Education And Later Relationship Help-Seeking', *Journal Of Family Psychology*, 2018

that men are less likely to seek help, especially for psychological issues, could the expectation of an equal, honest marriage be making men more self-aware, open and responsible about their psychological well-being?

Living In, Marriage, Fatherhood and Beyond

'Oh, I cried when I saw my son for the first time. I cried so much!'

— Rajat, thirty-six

MARRIAGE, IN OUR culture, is the only respectable form of coupling. Without a religious or legal solemnization, a relationship doesn't hold much social standing. This sanctimonious union between two families is regarded as an initiation into adulthood for men and women. Until married, one is the responsibility of parents. Once you hit 'marriageable age', you go from being a responsibility to a liability. No credence is given to an individual who may be managing a job and a household impeccably. Unless bound in holy matrimony, one is essentially still a child running wild and free.

Wild and free... This stereotyped judgement has many grave implications for our mental and social health. While working on this book, I came across many men and women in their late twenties or early thirties who have had short-lived marriages and were coping with the repercussions of having failed the glorified institution that is seen as a reflection of one's morality, wisdom and character.

Jas, twenty-eight, had agreed to marry a girl of his family's liking through the arranged marriage set up, but he soon discovered that the incompatibility between the two was irreconcilable. Two years later, he is stuck fighting a messy legal battle and is in a limbo when it comes to his romantic life. His is one among many such stories. In India, marriage is considered a milestone, to be reached by a certain age. Many give in to this 'milestone' even though we may not be ready emotionally. School, job, marriage, kids — this is the trajectory that has been laid out for us. Any deviation from this blueprint is considered unorthodox at best and immoral, selfish and immature at worst.

That marriage is a greatly patriarchal system is indubitable. A traditional marriage, founded on the acquisition of the woman, is based on roles and responsibilities divided according to one's gender. The man brings home the bacon while the woman emotionally and gustatorily nurtures the family. The man pays the bills and ensures that the electricity, plumbing and other such foundational necessities of maintaining and running a house are met, and if necessary, plays handyman himself to do so. The woman buys the linen, stocks the pantry, decorates the walls and ensures that the house becomes a home. The man comes home to rest, to retreat from the hubbub of his life outside the home while the woman spends her days in the upkeep of a calm, safe and relaxed haven for the man to come back to. Sex is the man's prerogative — the reward he is entitled to for providing shelter and food for the woman he is legally responsible for. Female desire and pleasure do not figure in this dynamic for reasons that are multi-layered and complex.

Many problems arise in this traditional set up. Our generation's cynicism towards marriage and unwillingness to compromise in the ways that the generation before us did, is testimony to the dysfunctions of a gendered marriage. Women's financial independence has been one of the primary causes of the breakdown of this system. A mere functional partnership where tasks are delegated to ensure smooth running of the household and caretaking of the family seems to be on its way out. We want more. A thirty-one-year-old friend of mine, who is contemplating divorce after a four-year-long tumultuous marriage, tells me, 'I don't want to spend my life dealing with maids, going to all these family functions and fake smiling with someone I have only a working relationship with. That's what it is, isn't it? The Indian family that our parents treat as something marvellous…it's a working relationship; like you run a company together. I don't want that. Where's the love, man?'

While this disillusionment with gendered marriages is on the rise, there are a few things that have remained unchanged. The decision to get married still mostly lies with the man. After having spoken to several unmarried men, some who were dating casually and others who were in serious relationships, I began to suspect that men have a timeline with regards to marriage. They — not unlike the trajectory of education, job, marriage, kids — want to achieve certain goals before they take on the role of the husband. For many men, marriage was something they envisioned entering in their thirties even if they were already with the one they wanted to marry. Abhishek Kashyap calls this the 'financial clock'. He's of the opinion that most men want to be financially ready before they take the plunge. 'I didn't want to get married when I was making seventy to eighty thousand and living in Mumbai.'

Now as financial independence among women is being normalized and even becoming a necessity because of the ever-increasing cost of living, many men are setting this 'financial clock' for their partners too. Jaiwin has these goals for both himself and his girlfriend — both must be financially stable before they get married. Jacob's girlfriend works in the same industry as him, and this is a source of relief for him. From the wedding expenses to living expenses to future savings, everything is taken care of by both. 'I feel relieved. Otherwise, it would be too much of a burden on me,' he tells me.

With so much changing so rapidly in our society, the institution of marriage is under scrutiny like never before. It's not only the economic independence of women that has shaken the institution of marriage. On 26 October 2006, the Government of India enforced the Protection of Women from Domestic Violence Act. According to this act, any woman who is either threatened by or is subjected to any form of abuse — physical, emotional, sexual, verbal or economic — by a male she cohabits with, is entitled to legal protection from him. According to this Act, designed to secure housing for women, it is not only the lawfully wedded wife but any woman — a sister, mother, daughter or even a romantic partner — who shares a house with a man is entitled to be protected from violence. The implementation of this Act has inadvertently legalized live-in relationships, or rather, decriminalized them. In recent years, many cases have come to light where the judge in action has lawfully sanctioned consenting adults to cohabit with each other even if they are not wedded.[9] In fact, judges have been known to say that a man and woman living together will be considered married in the eyes of law and will be subjugated to the same rights and laws. In simple words, living-in may be considered morally dubious, but legally it is considered the same as marriage.

Consider the scenario about ten to fifteen years ago. Premarital sex was considered a sin and living in was an alien concept. I recall an incident in the apartment complex I grew up in circa 1996–2008. An urgent meeting was called by the angry and distressed members of the Residents Welfare Association (RWA) committee. The local chemist had reported that 'young kids' from the complex were coming in frequently to buy condoms. The grown ups were livid and had got together to discuss the 'crisis' at hand. Even to my teenaged, virginal self, that seemed strange. Shouldn't they be glad that these people were having safe sex? I wondered. Premarital sex was never illegal, but it was immoral. We've come a long way since. We understand that becoming sexually active may not always coincide with marriage. With this acceptance of premarital sex, living in has also become less taboo, at least in the big cities.

[9] Hittanagi, Rajesh, 'Live-In Relationship And Indian Judiciary', Legal Services India

For many couples on the fence about marriage or unable to balance between their modern aspirations and traditional expectations of their families, live-in relationships are a godsend.

Many couples who take this step regard it as a stepping stone to marriage. 'How can you be sure this is the person you want to marry unless you've lived with them?' was a common sentiment among the couples I spoke to, who had also chosen to cohabit before making a commitment, not because they were disillusioned with the idea of marriage but because they wanted to make the right choice.

It goes without saying that not all live-in relationships progress to marriage. But this is not because those who opt for cohabitation shun marriage. Some simply believe that it would be less damaging for a live-in relationship to break apart, than a marriage. They worry that if they marry the wrong person, they'd end up having to deal with a divorce. So, in essence, this upsurge of live-in relationships is not reflective of a fear of marriage, but rather of divorce.

Divorce is on the rise in our country. The statistics on the number of marriages breaking down, often within the first year, may vary by state, socio-economic status, and religion, but it is an upward trend.[10] Times are changing. We no longer live in a society where women are willing to remain subservient to the system. We are changing, at a very personal, individual level, and these individual changes where women choose to build careers and men

[10] Dutt, Apoorva, 'How and Why Number of Young Indian Couples Getting Divorced Has Risen Sharply', *Hindustan Times*, 4 January 2015

look forward to building homes, not just houses — are beginning to cause ripples at the social level. Yes, marriage is breaking down. But, perhaps, only the traditional form of marriage.

Back in the day, 'family' meant living in a joint set up, with a set of grandparents, parents, uncles and aunts. As people migrate to urban centres, states, or the country itself, in pursuit of more prosperous opportunities the big, fat Indian family is no longer the norm. It has been replaced by the nuclear family, comprising husband, wife and children, and perhaps, ailing, aged parents. But it wasn't until women started joining the workforce and attaining financial independence that marriage itself started transforming in an unprecedented manner. Until a generation ago, women would not leave unhappy or abusive marriages because they would not have a place to go. Being financially dependent on your spouse, with no skill, education or work experience to help you stand on your own two feet meant that you had handed over your life to the man. That was just the way. Things are different now. Women can walk away from a bad marriage because they have the means to support themselves. Of course, many, if not most, still find it difficult to do so due to lack of family support or social stigma, but the trend is on the rise. Men have it relatively easier. Enter technology — specifically social media and dating apps — and a whole new world of options and access opens up! The collectivistic structure of our society is weakening, and personal ambitions are taking the forefront. Needless to say, marriage, which has so far relied on upholding cultural expectations over one's own personal desires, is suffering.

This breakdown of marriage is reflected not only in the rising cases of divorce. Widespread infidelity is another symptom of how marriage may be surviving on life support. In Delhi, you are better off assuming that someone you meet is either already attached to someone else or will attach themselves to someone else, unless exclusivity is explicitly talked about. In Jaipur, I hear from multiple sources that 'everyone's having an affair'! According to a survey conducted by Ashley Madisson, the notorious website for married individuals looking for thrills, 65 per cent of men and 77 per cent of women in Mumbai didn't think affairs were immoral![11] The reasons in each city may vary, but disloyalty is no longer considered to be a mortal sin. When you pay attention to the stories — the common reasons behind cheating today — you begin to realize that infidelity is not the problem but a symptom. The problem is the compulsion to marry and the disgrace attached to divorce.

Akshita, thirty-two, has been married for seven years and has a five-year-old son. She meets her lover — eight years younger to her — at fancy hotel rooms. They met at a bar one weekend while Akshita was out for some downtime with her girlfriends. When I ask her what this means to her, she keeps it simple, 'Attention, what else? He dotes on me so much; he's almost obsessive about me. But my husband...it's like he doesn't even see me. Especially since we had the kid.' How about addressing it with the husband, trying to fix the issue? I ask. 'I tried, but we never really had any communication. It

[11] Kamal, Hassan M., '65% Men, 77% Women In Mumbai Don't Think Infidelity Is Immoral', *Mid-Day*, 14 October, 2014

was an arranged marriage. One year after I got married, I got pregnant…after that, there's no time left to build a relationship even if you want to.' I ask her if she feels guilty. She shakes her head as she takes a long sip of her coffee. 'But if my husband ever finds out, he will kill me.'

Our society is plagued by loneliness. This model of marriage is fast becoming redundant for a generation that's challenging the status quo. We are caught at a crossroads and there is bound to be upheaval. Even though dating is not taboo for the young folks in our country, many still opt for an arranged marriage or explicitly look for someone who will be accepted by their family. We may increasingly be okay with casual sex, but this is often at the cost of someone's feelings, as we try to find the balance between pursuing our modern proclivities and honouring the tradition we're born into. Amid this push and pull, guided by utter cluelessness, we find ourselves in an epidemic of infidelity and failed marriages.

But this is not entirely a bad thing. It's not marriage or love or commitment that's dying. This marks the beginning of an end to the idea of 'settling' for someone just because that's what one ought to do. It's being oppressed by your partner and the system that expects us to check marriage off a list. Of course, when we see bad marriages all around, some amount of skepticism is inevitable. But our generation also has more freedom and knowledge to make choices that are authentic to us as individuals, that serve our needs for belongingness and intimacy.

One can't blame young couples for wanting to first live with someone before they commit to marriage. That said, for some couples cohabitation is a matter of practicality and convenience. Ishika and Kush, both in their late twenties, work and live in Delhi but come from different parts of the country. After dating for about two years, they decided to rent an apartment together because it helped them manage their time. It was also a more financially viable option. 'We would have long, hectic working hours and would not get to see each other so much. We would end up spending nights at each other's houses because that's pretty much what our schedules allowed. So it made sense to just move in together. That way we could get to spend more time together — every night — without one of us having to go through the inconvenience of packing night clothes and work outfits for the day,' Ishika tells me. I ask them if marriage is on the cards and neither seem too keen. This is not because they are not fully committed to each other, but rather the contrary; they don't see the point in going through the hassle of marriage.

According to Kush, bringing families in at this point would needlessly lead to complications and expectations. 'We are together. We are happy. Maybe when we want to have a kid or we are ready to buy a house together, we'll think about marriage. Right now, I don't see what it could add to our relationship other than being answerable to the parents.'

Even though in the eyes of the law, a child borne of a cohabitation has the same rights as the child born to a married couple, most couples in live-in relationships don't want to have or raise a child without getting married.[12] I broach this with Kush. 'I didn't know

[12] Mahapatra, Dhananjay, 'Supreme Court: Children Born Of Live-In Relationships Are Legitimate', *Times Of India*, 24 April, 2014

that...' he admits and then pauses to reflect. 'Hmm...' he begins, 'I don't think our society is ready for that, to be honest. I mean we break the law daily. We don't care about the law here. It's about our beliefs. If I have a child and I'm not married, then my kid will not get the acceptance he or she should.'

Like cohabiting couples don't get the social acceptance they should. For many cohabiting couples, commitment, love and security are not correlated with marriage. Marriage is seen as a stamp of social sanction for the relationship but not as a symbol of its quality or worth. When I asked couples what made living in more challenging than marriage, they stated that it was the social taboo and family pressure.

When I first met Vivek, a lanky twenty-something working with an NGO for animal rights protection, he was vehemently opposed to marriage. Living with his girlfriend of three years who was older than him by four, he didn't see the point in the 'bourgeoisie' institution. Two years later, his views on marriage began to change. The relationship was getting serious and they were getting tired of fighting their family's pleas to 'make it official'. In an intimate ceremony, the previously anti-marriage couple became man and wife. Shortly after his wedding, I caught up with the couple over a few drinks. They seemed happy. 'Things are not much different than before,' Vivek begins. 'But now all that nagging from our families is gone. It's peaceful.'

Not all couples are open about their living arrangement with their families because of the backlash they anticipate. There are also certain functional benefits one gets by solemnizing one's relationship. A big one is renting a house. Though not a problem legally, many landlords are unwilling to lease out their property to unmarried couples because of the taboo attached to it. When Robin and his girlfriend were hunting for a house in Delhi, they got more rejections than houses they liked. When asked by potential landlords if they were married, they would idealistically respond with honesty. 'No, sir.' 'No, ma'am.' After house-hunting for over a month, they got tired of the rejections and decided to lie about their relationship status. Their current landlord thinks they are married and is very pleased to have such a pleasant young couple living in his home. 'So if we decide to get married we can't have any parties at our house,' Robin jokes.

Jas, still battling his divorce in court, has moved on. He is now seeing Neha, but theirs is a unique situation. The couple live with Jas's family. They run a content company together, and I meet them in their office. They have come in an hour before the staff so that they can give me their undivided attention. 'We are living like a married couple; there's no difference,' Neha tells me. 'She sometimes worries about her rights,' Jas adds. Neha smiles and nods in agreement, 'Sometimes, I get insecure. What are my rights if I am not his wife?' Jas tells us in between sips of tea, 'I tell her that I love her and that it doesn't matter whether we are married or not. To me, her rights are the same as a wife's. Marriage is just for the families. To put their worries at ease.'

We make our own rules in this country. Where there's love, it seems, there is no law of the land.

THE FUTURE OF MARRIAGE IS FOUNDED ON 'PARTNERSHIPS'

When I asked men and women what they want in a marriage, one word repeated itself often — 'partnership'. When I asked what they meant by it, I heard descriptions that sounded similar to a peer marriage.

> 'Someone I can have real conversations with and someone who understands who I am.' — Aadil

> 'I think it's important to have shared interests in a marriage. I love to travel and I want to be with someone I can share that with.' — Rachit

> 'The reason I fell in love with my girlfriend is because she can take charge of things. I don't have to be worried about her safety or do little things for her. She's very independent and makes me feel she can also take care of me if I need.' — Jacob

After the birth of their baby, Tushar's wife stopped working. It was necessary at the time. But now, while Tushar makes enough to be able to support the family, he wants her to get back to work. His wife wants to open a boutique but according to Tushar, she 'lacks the focus'. He doesn't care what she does as long as she does something. I ask him why it's important to him. 'I think my wife feels a little underconfident. If she starts working, I think she will become more sure [*sic.*] of herself. And with the baby, it will help to have another earning member. In case something happens to me, or I lose my job, there should be a back up.' Or a partner.

Not only do younger men want a partner who can share the financial load, they also want to be more hands-on around the house. In fact, they take pride in it.

Since the pandemic began, Pranav and his wife converted their guest room to an office and Pranav has been doing most of the cooking. 'Sometimes if I'm tired or not in the mood, I ask Ankita to cook. But I enjoy doing it. Before the lockdown I never had an opportunity.' Both Pranav and Ankita are foodies, so Pranav's culinary experiments are a source of joy and a topic of discussion in their home.

Aadil, though alone, has taken to gardening during the lockdown. He sends me pictures of the cherry tomato plant growing on his terrace garden. 'This is what I want when I get married,' he texts me. 'I want to be with someone I can listen to The Beatles with and plant trees with.'

Although most men still want to be able to make enough money to be able to provide their family with a good life and most women still leave their family homes and join the husbands', the equation is changing. Marriage in India is slowly becoming more egalitarian. This partnership that men and women are looking for in marriages goes beyond having a second source of income or sharing household chores. Like women, some men also want a partner they can connect with.

OPENNESS AND HONESTY ARE STILL A DISTANT DREAM

Tushar is still in touch with Mitali. 'I don't feel any guilt,' he tells me. 'I love my wife very much and I want to make her happy. But I have certain needs which are not fulfilled in my marriage.' These needs are purely sexual, he tells me. Other than a sex life, which Tushar finds too vanilla, he has a wonderful marriage. 'So this arrangement I have with Mitali helps me fulfil those needs, and I am satisfied now. I have a good home life and I don't let sexual frustration ruin my marriage. That's how I see it.' Tushar has split himself into two — one, the loving, kosher husband who doesn't complain when deprived of oral sex or dirty talk, and the other, the raunchy lover who can indulge in as much oral sex or dirty talk as he likes.

Karthik has split himself into many. He has a wife, who currently lives in another city and several women he dates and hooks up with. He, too, has no regrets. 'We give too much meaning to sex,' he explains in a pedagogical tone. 'It's just for the body, you see. It means nothing more. You see, monogamy came about only because of land. Humans wanted to own land, so that's how marriage started.' I ask him if he owns any land. He laughs. 'No, no, that's not…I mean to say monogamy is not natural for us.' I steer him to talk about himself — the personal, not the theoretical. As I do this, I'm reminded of a lesson I learnt early on while working on this book — men tend to use intellectualization as a defence mechanism to avoid confronting real issues. So what was Karthik trying to avoid?

Karthik got married because of family expectations. He and his wife are very different, he tells me. She comes from a traditional south Indian family and he, having travelled the length and breadth of the country, doesn't relate to those limiting values anymore. It's hard to keep Karthik focused on the personal. For every ten seconds he dips his head in the water, he needs to keep his head up to take deep breaths for ten minutes. The personal seems too scary for him. He'd rather talk at a theoretical level. So he explains to me that sex was never necessary for marriage and that there's nothing wrong with him sleeping with other women.

I figured if he's so certain about this, he must have convinced his wife of this idea by now. I ask him what his wife thinks about this. He shakes his head, 'Oh no no. She doesn't know. Ha ha.' A pause, and then, 'Actually she found out once. She was very angry, and it took a long time to make the situation better.' To convince his angry wife he was worthy of being her husband, he gave her access to all his bank accounts and investments and assured her he would always take care of her.

I asked both Tushar and Karthik how they would feel if their wives felt sexually dissatisfied in the marriage and wanted to be with someone else. The two men have nothing in common (except that both have daughters and both are cheating on their wives) — one had a love marriage, the other an arranged marriage. One grew up in a small town with frequent power cuts, the other grew up in a city. One is hooked to the world of dating apps; the other has never used any. One is an academician and the other, a corporate slave. One has one lover, the other has many. Their native languages are different too, and they've never lived in the same city. Never crossed paths.

Yet their answers were exactly the same.

'I wouldn't want to know if she was sleeping with someone else.'

WHAT HAPPENS WHEN MEN BECOME FATHERS?

Fatherhood seems to be a pivotal moment for most men. It makes them stop and reevaluate their lives quite unlike marriage. Becoming a father, to most, means reshuffling priorities.

'When I saw my daughter for the first time, my heart stopped,' Tushar tells me. 'She is the most beautiful thing in the world!' Tushar is enjoying every minute of parenthood. Although his wife takes care of feeding the baby and diaper changes, he chimes in wherever he can. 'She is the centre of my world. I'll give anything for her happiness.'

Karthik is trying to be a better person for his three-year-old daughter. 'I still want all this with other women, I'll not lie, but I don't want my daughter to grow up watching her parents fight with each other. So I am more careful now. I avoid it [the affair] if I think my wife will find out.'

For Suraj, the lockdown has given him an opportunity to be with his son. 'I never spent this much time with him before. He's four now and he's fairly independent. Priyanka has done a good job with him. But now I realize what I've missed — I wasn't here when he walked for the first time or spoke his first words. Now that I see what a smart young boy he is, I don't want to miss out on these moments.'

Urban Indian fathers are invested in the cognitive and social growth of their children. In Hindu families, according to a paper published in the *Journal of Family Issues*, this includes passing on *sanskaars.*[13] Some young fathers, however, feel excluded from the process of parenting. There are several obstacles to this. One is the lack of paternal leave in our country and the second is the way young fathers are sometimes excluded from child rearing by other family members.

Thirty-six-year-old Vishrut, a professional working in Singapore, is dad to a seven-month-old baby girl. I meet them at Vishrut's older sister's house where they are visiting from Singapore. His wife and he moved to Singapore shortly after their wedding three years ago and haven't yet assimilated to the culture there. Their daughter is cheerful and friendly and doesn't seem to cling to her mother very much. She wants to walk around the living room, pick up things from the table and put them on the floor. Her mother can't take her eyes off her daughter though. I ask Vishrut about fatherhood and he tells me it's a steep learning curve for him. 'I think caretaking comes more naturally to women. She,' he points at his wife, 'just knows how to hold the baby or clean her or feed her. These things are very hard for me. I try to learn, though.' He then draws an analogy for me. 'I think dads are like nurses — they assist the mom who's the real doctor here.'

---

[13] Sriram, Rajalakshmi, Sandhu, Gurprit Kaur, 'Fathering to Ensure Child's Success: What Urban Indian Fathers Do?', *Journal Of Family Issues*, 2012

It's time for their daughter's diaper change. Vishrut offers to do it. His older sister says, 'No it's okay, you leave it. I'll do it, it will be quicker.'

In many Indian households, including Tushar's and Karthik's, a large part of child rearing is taken care of by women — mothers, grandmothers, aunts. We presume that the mother–child bond is supreme and that fathers aren't capable of taking care of the child like mothers. Other than breastfeeding, which is also difficult for many women, there is no caregiving that men are less capable of compared to women. It's just that we don't allow them into the space.

Ask a man to describe the moment he first laid his eyes on his child and you'll realize that men have hearts too.

When I asked Rajat this, he said, 'Oh, I cried when I saw my son for the first time. I cried so much!' When Rajat and his wife were expecting a baby in the US, he was also instructed by the doctors on how to look after the newborn. 'I was told to hold the baby to my chest without a shirt on. That daily skin-to-skin contact is recommended for fathers.' Rajat took a four-month long paternity leave when his son arrived. During these four months, he and his wife were hands-on with the baby. Rajat helped change diapers, feed and burp the baby; he did everything many Indian men think they 'can't' do as well as mothers.

Rajat Mittal is an Indian man who grew up in a small town where boys and girls weren't allowed to talk to each other and where men didn't provide care or emotional support. He studied engineering and was raised with lessons such as 'boys don't cry' and 'men must provide'. He was well on his path to becoming the man of patriarchy's dreams — financially stable and successful in a male-dominated field. Yet, here he is, changing his baby's diapers, holding him to his chest and through his personal and professional life, changing gender norms.

In the end, I've learned that masculinity in modern love is about the choices that men make.

AFTERWORD

When a large number of individuals from one demographic group exhibit similar behaviour, it becomes more than individual behaviour. It becomes the behaviour of the group. Listening to women's stories of modern love and heartbreak, I noticed several such behaviours that seemed to be common among many men — rather, common in their treatment of women. Being uncomfortable with the woman's past relationships; dictating if and how the relationship will progress (and when); avoiding confrontation about their behaviour while holding the women to a high standard; deflecting attention from uncomfortable topics; getting impatient with, or being uninterested in things that don't directly serve them; treating sex as an activity void of any emotion or connection. In the wake of #MeToo, this pattern among men of treating women as objects, properties or, as I learnt, 'achievements', became all the more clear. Like any other woman, I want to line up all the men in a row, and tell them to stop this atrocious behaviour. But, one can't change something without first understanding why it happens.

When I began working on the book, I believed that there were two types of men — men who believed in gender fluidity in relationships, honesty and loyalty; and those who didn't. Quite black and white, I'll admit. When #MeToo happened, this belief was shaken to the core. Since those first few rude shocks of men I'd previously thought were sensitive and respectful toward women, being called out during the movement, my worldview of men has become all grey. And I haven't gone back since.

This grey area, though, has benefited the book greatly. Through this book, I have discovered and tried to highlight the dichotomies among young men in our country today — the loving boyfriends and husbands who want a fling on the side; the charming, kind and attentive men on dating apps who are confused about what they want; those who want their partners to excel but feel inadequate when they themselves aren't providing; the aloof, mysterious ones who in fact, crave strong connection; the men who hold their stoicism in high regard, even though they may be aware that it makes them emotionally inaccessible to the women in their lives. Like our country itself, masculinity, and modern love are rapidly changing, and men are stuck in this cultural quagmire, trying to find the best way out.

When I first began speaking to men, I suspected they wouldn't be as open as they were. I suspected they would give me politically correct answers, and — to use a modern romance term — 'wokefish' me. Instead, I found myself becoming a sounding board for many men who were themselves trying to navigate this new world of changing gender norms. The urgency with which some men shared their stories confirmed my initial hypothesis — that men and women weren't talking to each other enough; and that men wanted to put their stories out there. I also became privy to the angst some men face because of the uprising of spotlighting women's lives. I wonder — in wanting to make women more visible, are we inadvertently making men less visible?

I have been wary of coming across as an MRA — men's rights activist. In fact, it's my most dreaded fear that this book will be received as an anti-women, pro-men book. It's neither of these. It's simply a commentary on what's on the minds of modern men. Unless we understand their narrative, we are shooting in the dark. For this reason, as much as possible, I have tried to showcase men's stories in light of women's issues. To put it in context.

When Pradyum — after a few enthusiastic interactions — stopped interacting with me, the first thought that came to my mind was that he, like so many other men, had a life that was hidden from his partner. His silence has screamed loudly in my mind, and when I tune in to listen to it, I hear a different story — Pradyum is a duty-bound family man who, at the same time, has his own story to tell and no one to tell it to. His is a story of sacrifice, of giving in to his family's expectations of a marriage that carries forth their traditions. For him, his family's happiness is supreme. Before he became a married man, his priority was to make his parents happy. Now, it's his wife. But he challenged this status quo when it was time for his younger sister to get married. She, with his support, became the first in his family to marry someone of her choosing. He put his own resentment aside for the happiness of his sister, so she wouldn't have to make the same sacrifices he had to make. I imagine he'd have done the same for a brother. His silence, and negation of me when he said 'I don't want my wife to know I'm talking to a Prachi,' was not about him or me. It was about his wife's happiness.

Karthik staunchly believes that sex and love mustn't be confused. He is knowledgable, and can recommend several books that support his philosophy of modern love. He wishes his wife had had a chance to explore who she is and what she believes in, and doesn't want his sister or daughter to be boxed in by social expectations. He is close to his sister, he tells me, and learnt a lot about how to behave around women from her. 'I didn't know my some things I did would make women uncomfortable till my sister told me,' he had said. He had a smile on his face throughout our conversation. He's a happy man, he says. But I wonder if his desire for his sister and daughter to not be boxed in by social expectations, is a desire for himself.

The most important factor for solving any relationship issue is communication. But, how can we communicate with someone else, if we don't communicate with ourselves? How can we be honest with another, if we aren't first brutally honest with ourselves?

Opposite sex friendships are absolutely necessary for humanising the other sex; for men and women to see each other as whole beings with aspirations and disappointments. For this reason, I've always had a visceral reaction against boys' only or girls' only groups, boys vs. girls games, or mens' only and women's only activities. In many Indian families even today, get togethers mean that at some point, the men will segregate in one area and the women in another.

The men may talk shop or politics. Maybe they'll smoke or drink. The women will talk about domestic affairs. Maybe they'll start preparing the food that's to be served soon. I don't know. I've never stayed long enough at one of these to find out. But, I have walked away from many of these growing up in my family, and even today, when I see it — in my family or someone else's — I shudder. I react with all my body and soul, and want to projectile vomit. I have the same reaction when I see groups of friends segregating based on their assigned sex.

For a while a few years ago, I tried to experiment with it. To exclude boys from girls' night outs, plan girls' only trips, so on and so forth. It's all the rage on the internet — #girlsquad, #girlpower, #whoruntheworld, #womensupportwomen. So, I figured, maybe there is real power in not allowing men into women's spaces, and I shouldn't dismiss it without first trying.

Women's only groups are non-threatening. We don't have to worry about that 'friend' making a pass at us after a few drinks, or be interrupted by that guy in the group who *thinks* he knows more. Women, when surrounded by other women, feel *safe.* Well, in most cases. If we're not worrying about being judged or shamed for what we wear, say, drink, eat, do, or think, we can be unencumbered. It is *empowering* to live like that. But, is that power? Let me put it this way — did making women's only compartments in Metros make the rest of public transportation any safer for women?

What happens when you get out of that bubble and go back to the real world where men and women share the same rooms, offices, restaurants, bars, colleges, wedding halls, hospitals, and other public places? And who has the power at home?

As things stand today, men and women don't co-exist in harmony. That co-existence, and meaningful sharing of both physical and cognitive space, will happen only if we befriend each other. I hope this book inspires you to do that.

ACKNOWLEDGMENTS

This book wouldn't be possible without the men and women who shared their stories and thoughts. First and foremost, I'd like to thank them. For their candour. Their unanswered questions and unasked for answers. Their jokes. Their book and movie recommendations. Their controversial opinions.

Prerna, for reminding me to keep the journalist hat on while I listened, and bringing out the best in me and this book.

Kanishka, for the vote of faith and friendship.

Ayush Chandra and Tanya Appachu, without whose professional inputs, this book would be incomplete.

My parents, for patiently sitting through readings that often lasted well past their bedtime, and then rating each chapter with stars (5 stars for all except Consent 101).

My brother Pikun, for those endless conversations about masculinity and love, over whiskey and wine. My sister-in-law Arpita, for challenging gender norms without dimming the light of love. Together, the two make for a pretty great peer marriage, reassuring me that it's not idealistic to expect it.

My niece, for saying it like it is, and reminding me that the solution to many of our adulthood problems might just be to go back to that childlike honesty.

And finally, my partner, Mohit, for comforting me through multiple breakdowns, leaving me alone when I needed to finish a draft, and jumping right in to give me a massage when I needed a break.

AUTHOR BIO

Prachi Gangwani is a Delhi-based writer and content creator. Currently, Gangwani adorns two hats: She runs a digital publication, Keeping Zen, which delves into relationships, sex and gender, and wellness. She is also the Content Lead at Human Edge Enterprises. After studying psychology and practicing as a family and couples counsellor for two years, Gangwani switched to a full-time writing career. She has worked with Scoopwhoop Media, iDiva (Times Internet Ltd.), Hauterrfly (Fork Media), and Juggernaut Books. Her words also appear in *DailyO*, *The Swaddle*, and *Asia Spa Magazine.*